STONE AND METAL VASES

STONE AND METAL VASES

SIR W. M. FLINDERS PETRIE

OXBOW | books
Oxford & Philadelphia

This edition published in the United Kingdom in 2024 by
OXBOW BOOKS
81 St Clements, Oxford OX4 1AW

and in the United States by
OXBOW BOOKS
1950 Lawrence Road, Havertown, PA 19083

Paperback Edition: ISBN 979-8-88857-073-9
Digital Edition: ISBN 979-8-88857-074-6 (epub)

First published by the British School of Archaeology in Egypt, 1937
Facsimile edition published in 1977 by Aris & Phillips Ltd

Oxbow Books is grateful to the Petrie Museum for their collaboration in bringing out these new editions

Printed in the United Kingdom by CMP Digital Print Solutions

For a complete list of Oxbow titles, please contact:

UNITED KINGDOM
Oxbow Books
Telephone (0)1226 734350
Email: oxbow@oxbowbooks.com
www.oxbowbooks.com

UNITED STATES OF AMERICA
Oxbow Books
Telephone (610) 853-9131, Fax (610) 853-9146
Email: queries@casemateacademic.com
www.casemateacademic.com/oxbow

Oxbow Books is part of the Casemate Group

Front cover: Black buff serpentine vase, height 107 mm, from Naqada Tomb T 16, Neqada II period (3500–3200 BC). Petrie Museum UC4355. Image courtesy of the Petrie Museum of Egyptian and Sudanese Archaeology, UCL.

CONTENTS

STONE VASES

INTRODUCTION

LIST OF PLATES

STONE VASES

METAL VASES

PREFACE TO THE 2024 EDITION

In the 1970s, a much-anticipated new series of publications illustrated objects and themes related to the excavations of the archaeologist William Matthew Flinders Petrie (1853–1942) in Egypt, and aspects of the collection of University College London's Petrie Museum of Egyptian and Sudanese Archaeology. A young couple setting up in business in the early 1970s, Aris and Phillips published these works, written by members of the UCL Egyptology Department, in their *Modern Egyptology* series. Building on Petrie's own observations, the authors of these volumes aimed to complete the great task of publishing the Petrie Museum of Egyptian and Sudanese Archaeology's vast collection, and to present some of the research that Petrie himself was not able to address in his own published works during his lifetime. As the current Curator of the Petrie Museum, it is a great privilege for me to support Oxbow Books in their mission to republish the series, which remains a key source of information for all those interested in object-based approaches to the study of the ancient world.

The Petrie Museum, part of University College London (UCL), is home to one of the largest and most significant collections of Egyptian and Sudanese archaeology in the world. Free to visit, this extraordinary collection tells stories about the lives of ordinary people who lived along the Nile Valley thousands of years ago. Originally set up as a teaching collection, the Petrie Museum comprises over 80,000 objects housed together with an internationally important archaeological archive. It is a collection of world firsts and 'oldests': the oldest woven garment; the oldest worked iron objects; the first known depiction of loom weaving; the oldest known written document about women's health; the earliest veterinary treatise; the oldest will on paper. The Museum has Designated Status from Arts Council England, meaning that it is considered to have outstanding resonance and national cultural significance. The collection has a substantial, visible international reputation for research, supporting hundreds of researchers every year, both remotely and in person.

The Petrie Museum is named after Flinders Petrie, who was appointed in 1892 as the first Professor of Egyptian Archaeology and Philology in the UK at UCL. Over three-quarters of the material in the Museum comes from excavations directed or funded by Petrie, or from purchases he made for university teaching. In 1880 at the age of 26, Petrie travelled to Egypt to survey the Great Pyramid. For the next five decades he was at the forefront of the development of archaeology in Egypt and later in Palestine, and his detailed methodological approach continues to shape the discipline today.

Petrie worked at more sites, with greater speed, than any modern archaeologist: seeing his life as a mission of rescue archaeology, Petrie aimed to retrieve as much information as possible from sites that were shrinking dramatically in size as Egypt modernised during the late 19th and early 20th centuries. He published a large part, but not all, of the finds from his excavations in his illustrated typological volumes, arranged according to object types and themes. Today, much of the Petrie Museum's collection is displayed and stored in a way which reflects these publications: for example, several storage cupboards are dedicated to the material illustrated in the 'Objects of Daily Use' volume, and objects in the drawers are arranged according to the order of the published plates. This offers a unique opportunity for researchers to engage with Petrie's typological and methodical approach to archaeology, as well as with the history of museum collections.

The first catalogue to be published in the *Modern Egyptology* series was *Amarna: City of Akhenaten and Nefertiti* in 1972 by Julia Samson, Petrie Museum Honorary Research Assistant. As official publishers to the UCL Egyptology Department the series went on to produce facsimile reprints of eight of Flinders Petrie's most important site reports and many of his object catalogues, originally published through the British School of Archaeology in Egypt. The substantial annual royalties from these reprints were paid into the 'Petrie Fund' at the time, which provided special grants to students in financial need.

In many ways, the new reprints of this classic series can be seen as the latest layer in a vast 'publication stratigraphy' of the thousands of finds from Flinders Petrie's excavations, which now live in museum collections around the world. On reading these volumes, I hope that readers will also be inspired to learn more about the Petrie Museum collection and its fascinating history.

Dr Anna Garnett
Petrie Museum of Egyptian and Sudanese Archaeology,
University College London
January 2023

PUBLISHER'S PREFACE

Oxbow Books is pleased to present this title in our *Classics in Egyptology* series. This series of facsimile re-issues is comprised of two sub-series. The first consists of 16 typological catalogues produced by W.M. Flinders Petrie based on his massive collection of Egyptian artefacts. Mostly excavated by Petrie during many seasons of campaign in the last years of the 19th and early decades of the 20th century, they now reside in the Petrie Museum at University College London. Published between 1898 and 1937 and long out of print, the catalogues were re-issued in facsimile by publishers Aris and Phillips in the 1970s. These were followed in the next 15 years or so by publication of a number of newly commissioned titles, based on more recent examination of elements of the Petrie Collection by contemporary experts, under the name *Modern Egyptology*. A selection of these additional titles forms the second component of our own series.

The archaeology of Egypt continues to fascinate. Multi-disciplinary investigation and research continues unabated, encompassing methodologies, scientific and data processing techniques, theoretical approaches, and even whole paradigms that were unheard of in the 1970s and undreamt of when Petrie was working in Egypt. Yet all the titles included in this series continue to be invaluable sources of basic data, providing an unparalleled resource that can easily be cross-referenced with the actual materials they describe and discuss. They remain within the Petrie Collection where they may be accessed and re-examined as new research flourishes. As historic documents, the Petrie catalogues stand as exemplars of the craft of typological classification, the backbone of modern archaeology – much of which, though refined by absolute dating and another 100 years of research, still stands the test of time.

A note on presentation

The facsimile titles of Petrie's catalogues re-issued in the 1970s were produced from scans of the original publications. Scanning technology at that time was not of the standard or resolution of today. The scans are no longer available, nor has it been possible to obtain, and in doing so destroy, original copies of the Petrie catalogues. These titles have therefore, of necessity, been rescanned from the 1970s re-issues. Where necessary the pages have been digitally enhanced for clarity of reading and to ensure the good quality of the plates, though inevitably a few are not of the standard we might wish, because of the quality of the previous scan, and occasional blocks of text are not precisely 'straight' or evenly situated on the page. However, some pages in the 1970s re-issues had been inserted in the wrong order and this has been corrected. The originals were produced at a folio size. The pages have been reduced slightly to standard A4 for ease of shelving and because this has the effect of slightly improving the scanned images. In some cases, illustrations were presented to scale and the original scale is given on the plate. There were also no digital files available for titles included in the *Modern Egyptology* series, so these too have been scanned from printed copies.

STONE AND METAL VASES

INTRODUCTION

1. In studying the stone vases, it seems best to set aside the prehistoric forms already described with other prehistoric remains in *Prehistoric Egypt* xxxiv–xlii. This course has been followed in other classes of objects; and as the vases are here dealt with in historical order, the separation of the earlier period does not break up the present arrangement. In several ways the prehistoric work is on a different footing from that of the dynastic times, and few types of vases run through from one age to the next. Where reference to earlier forms explains a type, they are briefly noticed here.

Previous publications on stone vases are of (*a*) disconnected groups in excavations, invaluable for dating but only touching one period; or (*b*) *corpus* lists according to form, essential for registering forms as found, and for descriptive purposes; or (*c*) the undated mixture of examples deposited in museums, with very rarely any history which can be of use for dating purposes. None of these provide for an historical view of each class of forms. To arrange the varieties of each general form historically is still requisite, in order to show the history of the types, the contemporary varieties, and the style of each period. The collection at University College, including most of the forms that are known, gives a fit ground for an historical treatment of the subject. This catalogue is therefore not merely a list of chance specimens, but is a first step toward a consecutive history of the forms and varieties of stone vases. Of the 728 examples in the Cairo catalogue, only half are drawn.

2. *Mode of dating.* Few of the vases here are absolutely dated; but every undated example has been compared with all dated vases that are published, and the nearest form that is found is stated in the text. This gives a tolerably close date for nearly all forms here, and they are arranged according to that order. A few uncertain forms are placed apart. I regret that the mixture of several periods of vases at the ruins of the temples of Menkaura precludes the use of that material here.

The dating of the vases and other remains is derived from various sources and by various methods. The most direct is the royal name on a vase, as on those from the ist dynasty, dedications of the ivth, vth, and vith dynasties, and the occurrence of later names, especially those of Tehutmes III, Amenhetep III, Ramessu II, and later the Bubastites and the Saites. Next are those found in royal tombs, or with named objects, such as scarabs, in groups. Then those associated in groups, or by levels, with objects dated from other sources, such as pottery. The mass of dated material, exactly published during the last fifty years, has left but few periods where there are not sufficient points fixed to determine the age of forms. The Ptolemaic and Roman periods are the worst known, owing to excavators having centred their attention upon papyri, and ignored the archaeology.

When we can deal with a closely dated series, such as the 700 forms from the royal tombs of the first three dynasties (*Royal Tombs* II, xxvi–liii G), each fixed to one reign, the changes in small features can be traced. We see how fashions were so short-lived that often some one detail is restricted to a single reign. This shows how needful it is to observe every detail of a form, and how minute the record of it must be, in order not to lose any possible result. Just as in experimental science a dozen attempts on different lines may be required before one of them yields a definite result, so here a great many details are found to have a wide range, and to be of little historical import. It is only by searching the whole field thoroughly that we can fix on those changes which are closely limited to one period. Even where there is some range of time for a form, it is useful to list all the instances, as in pl. XIII; thus, for instance, the cord pattern on cylinder jars is entirely limited to the range S.D. 78–81, except a very few early in the iiird dynasty, which might come from a previous source. The left-handed cord is only in 80–81. The cord is much commoner than the plain band in 78–80, the plain band is the more usual in 81, and is therefore the degenerate form. Thus the statistics of types, in each period that can be separately defined, is a further help. The most important group in this collection is that from the tomb of Neit-hetep, see pl. i, 1 to 9, nos. 12, 211 to 219, and 449.

3. *Illustrations.* For the comparison of details, photographs are inadequate; too often they are taken from a useless point of view, as the top view of a bowl; at the best, they give a skew view of either the top or base; and they never show the thickness and the interior form, which are very useful in discrimination. For comparison, it is only drawings that will suffice. These should, of course, always be made to a uniform scale; all my drawings of scientific value are already issued on a scale of $\frac{1}{3}$ for stone, being first drawn on $\frac{1}{2}$ and then reduced. This should therefore be adhered to for future publications. Where a collection can be dealt with all together, it is worth while to fix a rigid *camera lucida*. The greatest distance convenient for drawing is 26 ins. from the prism, the object being at 52 ins. for $\frac{1}{2}$ scale. A dotted outline should be made, so as not to hide the form by the pencil. Across the axis of the mouth of the vase, a straight-edge should be laid, and this defines the top accurately. After dotting the outline, the real drawing is made on the dots, finishing off the brim and base by observation and measurement. From three to six thicknesses, or inner widths, are measured, and the section line of one side drawn in. For small vases, under 4 ins., half of the above distances may be used, with a lens below the prism, so as to observe the form more exactly. For very large vases, the top and base can be drawn separately, shifting each opposite to the prism. Binocular drawing is much the best on long-distance work, keeping both eyes converged on the pencil, while one eye also sees the prism image. For drawing from fragments, see the stand in *R.T.* II, viii A.

The complete form should be drawn from a fragment, so far as may be possible. By measuring the diameter at one level, and reversing the fragment, each side can be drawn from it in relative position. If more than a quarter of the circumference remains, it should be put in a hollow right angle, and the radius read at the points of contact. Each drawing is completed here thus, so far as it can be. The slight irregularities in the drawings of the form are less than those of the actual vases, as each has been placed in the most symmetric direction for the drawing.

4. *Materials and forms.* In considering dates, the material has to be considered as well as the form. Some of the rarer rocks were only found once, and were used up in a reign or two. Thus large white-crystal porphyry was only used in S.D. 79, and perhaps 81: red porphyry is very rare in S.D. 79, and is never found again till Roman times; blue volcanic ash is limited to the ist dynasty; blue marble very rarely occurs after the xiith dynasty, though common then; purple fluorite is only known in the reign of Ramessu II. In smaller work, amethyst is scarcely ever found except in two periods, the xiith dynasty and Roman times; a long vein of it in granite, recently discovered, was probably the only source. Green noble serpentine and brown steatite are almost entirely prehistoric, and agate is of Greek times. Thus the material is often a clear guide to the date, and we should require the strongest evidence to date a translucent diorite vase outside of the iiird to vith dynasties. The source has been found in western Nubia.

In the origin of the forms of stone vases, there is less to be said than in the origins of pottery. Most of the types are obviously suitable for stone working, and in few instances does other material seem to have affected them. The cylinder jars are clearly a translation of pottery forms, which already had a long history before they appeared in stone. The bowls with recurved brims of the iiird–ivth dynasties may probably be derived from pottery forms then used. We happen to know of the common kohl pot form in glazed pottery earlier than in stone, but it may not have originated in pottery. Otherwise the stone forms seem to be quite independent, although a general resemblance can be seen between them and the pottery, as a matter of fashion, in each period.

5. *Manufacture.* The mode of manufacture was usually by grinding. The form was first chipped roughly, and the surface then worked down by emery blocks. The direction of grinding was not circular, but diagonal, on prehistoric vases. On the dynastic bowls, the grinding was done circularly in a block. For hollowing the interior, many methods were followed, according to the form. The main resource was to drill out a large core from the axis, to begin with; this removed the portion which would grind away most slowly, and left a hollow into which the sludge of grinding would fall. The main part was then ground out with a block, fed with sand or emery.

In the earlier part of the ist dynasty, the circular groove of the tube drill was carefully ground away in hollowing the interior. By the middle of the dynasty it was often left, showing as a ring in the smooth hollow. Later still, this ring mark was regarded as necessary, and was imitated by a scraped line if not already there. The means of hollowing undercut spaces, as in bowls with incurving edges, or vases with necks, is not clearly shown. Narrow bars were slipped up the axis of a vase and then turned across it, and were twisted round by a forked stick; for this purpose they were often of hour-glass shape. The forked stick, with a weight on the top to press the grinder down, became the usual hieroglyph for the word workman. There must have been a series of such grinders of increasing lengths; in some instances they are shown by the irregularities inside, as in xxiii, 581. The undercutting in bowls is a difficulty; apparently a grinder in two pieces must have been used. The difficulty of hollowing was well managed at first, as in xxi, 477, 488, leaving an almost uniform thickness. Later on, the hollowing was perfunctory, until it becomes merely ceremonial (iv, 57) or disappears altogether. An evasion of the difficulty began in the ist dynasty, by making a vase in two halves as xx, 451, 452, and this continued to be done in the xiith dynasty, xxiv, 627, 629, 632.

I have to thank Prof. Kosaku Hamada for kindly drawing the series of kohl vases 679 to 769 during his first visit to England in 1915. These were drawn full size, and are here reduced to 1 : 2.

CHAPTER I

THE CYLINDER JAR

6. *Derivation.* This is perhaps the only class which is clearly descended from prehistoric times. Early in the second prehistoric civilisation, large globular jars of pottery were made, with a ledge at each side half-way up, to serve as handles. This type became more upright, and the handle-ledges became wavy. In this form it survived for long in Palestine. In Egypt the wavy handles dwindled, the form gradually became cylindrical, the handles became a band of arched pattern, and passed into a mere ridge. In the earliest historic times, the ridge was notched as a cord pattern, decayed into a row of dots, and disappeared; the pot then dwindled, until by the end of the ist dynasty it was a little tube like a finger-stall. The stages of a wavy handle, a wavy ridge, and a cord pattern were all copied in stone; and the latter two, as figs. 1–11 show, belong to the historical age that we deal with here. The form then continued in stone, passing from a cylinder to a trumpet mouth in the xiith dynasty, as 127. Thus there was a change from globular sides to deeply concave sides, during a period of about 3,000 years. Archaistic copies (133 to 142) were continued for ceremonial use, for about 2,000 years later; this is the longest history of continued derivation that is met with in archaeology. The earlier part of it appears in full detail in the *Corpus of Prehistoric Pottery*, xxviii–xxx.

7. *Changes.* The history of the changes of detail can best be seen in pl. xiii, where the total of published examples, that are dated, are listed under each variation and period. In the last column, the numbers with + prefixed are added from the plates here. In the forms of brim, the cusp brim (A), and round brim (B), continue side by side through the ist dynasty, but the rounded brim is occasionally found later. The obtuse-angle brim (D) is peculiar to Kho-sekhemui. The thin parallel projecting brim (F to J) begins from the rounded type (F) under Neter-khet, and is the only form of the ivth to xiith dynasties, becoming much exaggerated, and then receding in the xiith dynasty. In the forms of body, the widening downward (B) is mostly of S.D. 78, but lasts to S.D. 81. The plain cylinder, or that with slightly hollowed sides (D, E), was usual from the beginning to beyond the middle of the ist dynasty, S.D. 78–81, and then suddenly passed into the concave-side form which started at 79, became commonest at 81, and lasted on to the iird dynasty. It became more deeply hollowed (M) at the end of the ist dynasty, and continued thus to the vith dynasty. The splay out to a foot at the base (N) seems to have started in the iird dynasty, and became the usual type in the vth and vith dynasties. Associated with a sort of flange projection at base and brim (O), this was the special vith dyn. form, surviving till the xiith dynasty. Lastly, the upper part became almost a conical trumpet shape (P).

The cord pattern also went through continual changes. The large wavy band is mostly late in dyn. O = S.D. 78, but survived into the time of

Mer-neit, S.D. 81. The small wave band had a shorter history, S.D. 78–80. The faint wave was more usual, from 78–81. The notched wave band was a degradation at 79, 80. The plain cord line belongs to the age of plain cylinder forms, beginning in 78 and ending in 81 ; various modifications of it appear in the same range. The left-handed cord is only of 80, 81. The plain band is of the same age as the common cord band. The cylinders without a band are known from S.D. 78, they become commoner till 81, and are universal after the ist dynasty, with the exception of a few cord patterns early in the iiird dynasty.

A correction should be stated here. Early in the work of classifying the prehistoric remains, the cylinder jars were dated (in *Diospolis Parva*) far back in the prehistoric series. This was due to my being supplied with reports of burials which were of mixed periods, without distinguishing the primary and secondary interments. Soon after that publication, I found the true position of the cylinders, in the tombs of the ist dynasty.

In the present account, only the more notable matters will be mentioned. The complete catalogue of the material, the nearest comparison of dated examples, the earlier publication and origin if known, and the date (known or inferred), appear listed further on in this volume.

8. *The early dynasties.* Pl. VI. The separate wavy handles still survived in the time of the obscure kings just before the ist dynasty, and such are therefore included here in the historical series. No. 1 is a portion of a magnificent jar, which is dated to S.D. 77 by the finding at Tarkhan ; but the same form of wave survived to the age of Neit-hetep, presumably the second reign of the ist dynasty. 3 has the wavy handles treated as serpents, a form not known elsewhere ; there is no trace of this being a modern adaptation, it appears to be entirely ancient. 6 is absolutely dated to the reign of King Ka, in dynasty O, before Mena, as it was found at Tarkhan with inscribed vases of Ka. This may perhaps be more truly classed with the small-handled vases in *P.E.* II, xxxix, 81, 85. No. 8 has a coarse imitation of the wavy band, made by cutting into a broad band, alternately above and below. In 9, the bulging sides occur at Tarkhan in 77 (type 51a) and 78 (type 51p), and in the tomb of Zer (*R.T.* II, liii, 362) in 79. The wide wave band occurs in 79 (*R.T.* II, lii, 348), and in 80 (*Tarkhan* i, type 51t), but never in the Gizeh tomb under Zet. This can hardly be dated otherwise than S.D. 79. 12 is a basalt jar of the series with similar markings, xi, 211–219, and xx, 449. Another vase that I have seen with this mark bore also the name Neit-hetep, and the forms of these would all agree with the date of that queen. It seems therefore probable that all of these marks were found in the royal tomb of Neit-hetep, excavated by De Morgan.

Pl. VII. From 16 to 25, these belong to the age of King Zet, S.D. 80. Fine concave outlines were beginning to prevail. These were carried to an exaggerated slenderness in the next reign, that of Den, S.D. 81, as in fig. 26. Pl. VIII. The plain band, or absence of band, increased during the reign of Den. One of the earliest vases with a private name is 37, with the inscription of the " Sacred scribe Safekht-nezemt." This name, " sweet is the goddess of writing," suggests that he came of a family of scribes. The vase is of gypsum, the softest of stones, which began to be used in this reign. Pl. IX. There appears a general decadence during the long reign of Den, like that in the reigns of Amenemhat III, and Amenhetep III, in later ages. The vases are largely plain instead of corded, and very coarse thick forms become common, as 50 to 60 ; the brims also are not well rounded, but there is often merely a flat space left between the inside and outside. A form somewhat like 53 recurs in the xviiith dynasty (*A.C.W.* III, xliv). Gypsum also became largely used, in place of the harder Egyptian alabaster. A great number of vases of this clumsy type were found in the excavations at El Kab. Pl. X. The angular brim, as 66, or bluff slope, 67, 68, 69, 71, 73, 75, are characteristic of the iind dynasty. The form is hardly defined in the rough model, 62, from the tomb of Qa. A peculiarly wide type occurs at Gizeh, dated to Neter-en, like 65 ; and 63, 64 are probably contemporary. For the late iiird dyn. date of the small cup-hollows, see *M.M.* xxiv, 11–15.

Pl. XI. **9.** *The ivth to vith dynasties.* The absolutely dated material is scanty for so flourishing a period. The temple of Menkaura, where most has been found, was so much altered and turned over that no vases can be dated thence. The tombs that have been opened have seldom been completely published, so the chance of getting fully dated objects after this catalogue was drawn up has been gladly secured. Especially is this needed for the characteristic form of the brim. Here we have 93A, a vase of Khufu for the early ivth dynasty, another of Teta 93B for the vith, and a third of

Pepy I 93C for the vith. The increase in width and reduction in thickness are clearly defined, seen in pls. IIA and XI, with the Khufu inscription repeated below in different light. The clumsy form in *L.D.* II, ii, 2, belongs to the series of thick alabaster, like vith dyn. types; but the equal curvature from top and from base belongs to the iiird dynasty, as 37, 71, and is not found in the vth dynasty or later. It seems therefore as if it must be assigned to the ivth dynasty. Nos. 78, 79 are also to be provisionally put to the ivth dynasty; but the whole of this part of the history will need to be written whenever the existing material is made of scientific use by a full publication. It may then appear that some examples now assigned to the iiird or vth may be of the ivth dynasty.

Narrow conical forms with a very sharp foot, 80–86, seem to be typical of the vth dynasty, and to extend to the vith. For these dynasties there are good dating points in the vases dedicated by kings, which have increasingly wide brims, as in that of Khufu 92A, wider under Teta, and more in 93 of Pepy I here; similar vases of Pepy and of Mer-en-ra are in Cairo Museum. The brim and base were both exaggerated at this period, sometimes absurdly, as in the beautiful diorite vase 95. This style continued in the decay of the Old Kingdom, as in 97, like a vase of about the ixth dynasty. The graceful curve of the sides was sometimes lost as in 98, like a vase of about the xth dynasty; and 103, 104 resemble this clumsy form in the xiith dynasty. It may be that 94 should come into the xth–xiith dynasties, owing to the clumsy body, and its being of a grey variety of the xiith-dynasty blue marble; but it is left here to the vith dynasty on the grounds of its brim and base. 96 was much like it, but the brim and base have all been broken away. The broad brim and foot lasted to the xith dynasty; see Antefaqer in *Dendereh* xxii.

10. *XIIth dynasty.* Pl. XII. The latest stage of the cylinder vase is the prevalent form in the xiith dynasty, with a small brim and less foot. The sets of six or seven of these vases are found in the tombs of this age, supposed to contain the unguents needful. Such sets are figured on the coffins, and bear sometimes the names of the different ointments. The original pottery jars that lead to the cylinder type were always for ointment; mud was substituted later, or the jar left empty. Serpentine was the favourite material, speckled, of black and dark grey, or of black and brown, or shades of dark brown. The blue marble of this age, and alabaster, were also used. Lids, which sometimes appear in the vith dynasty and onward, were usual at this time. Blue paste—imitating lazuli—also began to be used, as in the large vase 127. 129 may be derived from this type; it is dated to the xiith dynasty by its polish and thinness and its discovery at Kahun. It contained resin. By comparison of form, we must place 128 with this; but I should be more inclined to credit it to the ist dynasty. No. 130 I greatly suspect of being a modern attempt; but it is worked so thin, and entirely by hand, without a lathe, that it is kept here in case other examples should prove it to be ancient. It might be a clumsy local fabric of the ist dynasty. 131 is uncertain in age. 132 is of the xiith dynasty from Gizeh, with broken ivory wands. The following vases are all from foundation deposits, 133, 134 of Hatshepsut at Deir el Bahri, 135 of Tehutmes III at Amu (Kom Afrin), 136 of Tehutmes III at Nubt, 137, 138 of Tehutmes III at Koptos, 139 of Amenhetep II at Nekhen (El Kab), 140 of Amenhetep II naming Amen going sailing on the Nile, 141 of Amenhetep II at Thinis (?), 142 of Amenhetep II from his funeral temple at Thebes. None of them are well hollowed, and they degrade until there is only a slight hole on the top. Those of Yuaa under Amenhetep III are of the form 127, with a rather more splayed foot; this suggests that 127 may be of the xviiith dynasty.

CHAPTER II

BOWLS, STANDS, AND HANDLED VASES

Pl. XIII is a key to the dating of details of stone vases, with the number published of each period.

11. *Stands.* The Egyptian usually sat on the ground or on a slight stool; hence he only required low stands for his cups and plates, just to keep them out of the dust. Pottery stands are common, from mere rings up to tall trumpet-shaped tubes 2 or 3 ft. high.

Pl. XIV. 143 is a bowl and stand in one piece; this is the only example of such a combination that I have met with, and I should therefore doubt its age, but as it has been hollowed by a large tube drill, this seems to prove it to be ancient. 144, 145 are stone stands made in imitation of the pottery forms, with triangular holes. It seems probable that this style is a copy of stands made with crossing sticks, bound together and plastered with mud. 144 is absolutely dated to the iiird dynasty, being found in the ruins of the lower temple of Sneferu at Meydum. 145 is a fine piece of work in grey volcanic ash, drilled out from the base and the top. 146 appears to be a tray, rather than a dish, from the large diameter and flatness of it.

147 to 153, the low table stands, appear in the earliest examples at S.D. 81 (confirmed by the tomb of Den's vizier), but the greater part are of the iiird dynasty ; 149 and 152 in diorite are probably of the ivth dynasty. They thus seem to have a very limited range. The earlier forms, of the beginning of the ist dynasty, are rectangular with one end rounded, and three very short legs below (*P.T.* II, i, 3 ; *P.T.* I, xi, 23).

The earliest here is the low base, 148, on which a disc table has been cemented ; this is of S.D. 81. No. 147 may be as early, as there is a rather clumsier table of 81 (*Tarkhan* I, type 5m).

12. Pl. XV. *Handled vases.* The low vase with the two handles was one of the regular types of stone vase of the Gerzean prehistoric age, usually like 155, but with a flat brim. It was also largely imitated in pottery, painted to imitate stone patterns. This type certainly descended to S.D. 81, as 156, 158, and 166, from the Tarkhan cemetery, are of that age. As the others, from 154 to 159, are more like the dynastic than the prehistoric forms, they are included in this series. That the type was familiar in the early dynasties is proved by the very coarse and slightly hollowed examples found in the iiird dynasty, like 157 and 168. The idea of the type lasted down to the xiith dynasty, as seen in no. 160 of blue marble, and 161 from Harageh. Another type of the later prehistoric age, 169 to 178, is probably derived from the barrel vase with handles. Many were found at Naqadeh from S.D. 71 onward, like 169, 170, which I should place about S.D. 75. No. 171 is a type known to extend to 76. Nos. 172 and 173 are types of S.D. 77. No. 174 has been cut down anciently. 175 is a type of 78, and 177 is dated to S.D. 78. No. 176 seems to be of this date or earlier. The type lasted on to the vith dynasty, as shown by 178 from Zaraby. But none have been found in the iiird dynasty at Beyt Khallāf nor at Gizeh, nor any in the royal tombs of the ist and iind dynasties. The type was therefore practically extinct by the beginning of the ist dynasty.

13. Pl. XVI. *Bowls of ist dyn.* This is the largest class of all the stone or pottery vases. The bowl is often represented as held by the base in one hand while drinking from it. It is not so often found in the prehistoric ages, but is very common in the ist dynasty. The thousands of fragments of slate and alabaster bowls comprise the bulk of all that is found in the early royal tombs. The varying forms of the brim and of the inside base are tabulated with their dates in pl. xiii.

Pl. XVI. The examples that may be assigned to S.D. 77, 78, and 79 (that is, dynasty O and Mena) are placed together here, as it is difficult to distinguish them. There are several of fixed period, as 183, 184, found with pottery inscribed for Nar-mer, and 180, 185, 186, 189, 190, 191, 192, 196, 201, and 202 from the great deposit of Hierakonpolis. Two of these (201–202) bear the name of the Scorpion king of the Anu and one (196) that of King Ro. Others are dated by pottery in the graves at Tarkhan, as 195–200 of S.D. 77 ; nos. 179, 182, 187, 199, and 205 of S.D. 78, besides 209 like one from royal tombs of S.D. 79. The last named has been a magnificent bowl of red porphyry, ribbed, one of the very few objects of this stone before Roman times ; only the base and fragments of the sides and edge remain. Some intermediate examples are omitted from the drawings, as two dishes between 190 and 191 from Hierakonpolis, while a set of eight small funerary models varies between 193 and 194. The deep conical bowls are a feature of this period, and such as 206 is, for the size, thin cutting, and polish of it, a noble example of work.

The series of bowls 211 to 219 were bought, together with the cylinder jar 12, and the tall vase 449. The group of signs on all of them shows three fishes with heads toward a tank, and three objects behind them. The same group is on a cylinder in Berlin (*Z.A.S.* xxxiv, 160), and I have seen another such bowl with the name of Neit-hetep added. Probably all of these come from De Morgan's tomb of Neit-hetep at Naqadeh. On 214 there are also the marks of a square and a branch, well known in pottery marks. The two mouth signs on no. 210 show that this is one of a series with those bearing two mouth marks, along with numbers, which appeared on about a dozen prehistoric vases of various ages, offered to me all together. I carefully examined them, and the vases were clearly ancient ; but the numerals were greater the larger the vase, whereas the mouth means a fraction, and the number should be higher, therefore, on the smaller vases. I concluded that there was no proof of age in the marks themselves, that they were contrary to correct usage of such numerals, and that this discrepancy left no chance of the marks being ancient. It is needful to state this, as these marked vases have been adduced as evidence of the prehistoric use of hieroglyphs. The buyer must be incessantly on guard against forged or faked objects in Egypt.

Pl. XVII, S.D. 79–80. Reigns of Zer and Zet. The period of S.D. 80 is briefer than those before or after it, but is numbered apart, as it has a distinct character in its style. The recurved outline at the base of the bowl is seen earlier in some instances, 215 to 218, but it is usual in this period, as in nos. 225, 230, 233, 239, 240, and 245. It belongs to the refined style of Zet, seen in the hieroglyphs of the reign, and it is very seldom found in the coarser profusion of the reign of Den.

Pls. XVIII, XIX, S.D. 81, reigns of Den and Azab. This group includes also the age of the tomb of Mer-neit, the queen who died some years before Den. A new feature of the time is the use of very thick dishes with a central drill hollow, as 251, 252, and often with thick square edge, as nos. 253, and 255 to 259. The oval bowls 264, 265, 266 are of the ist dynasty, by the example of the dated pottery, S.D. 79–81, and they are too irregular in work to belong to the previous reigns. The fragment of a great bowl, 277, is placed here because the nearest parallel to the form is from the tomb of Den ; but the large-crystal porphyry would point to the beginning of the dynasty. The incurving of the edges is also another feature which, though starting before, now rules the style of the bowls, both in the flat forms 293 to 298, and in the deep forms 299 to 303. The latter begin the class which is so marked under Khosekhemui, xvi, 340–346.

Pl. XX, S.D. 82. The last two reigns of the first dynasty are much alike in products, and their separation is almost impossible owing to Amélineau having thrown the contents of one tomb into the other. The turning in of the edges progressed, and became extreme in some cases, 327, 328, like bowls from the tomb of Qa.

14. *Bowls of iind and iiird dyn.* Pl. XXI, iind dynasty. The style of the reign of Neteren is shown by a tomb dated with seals of Neteren at Gizeh. The peculiarity of the bowls of this reign (329 to 333) is the very wide sloping face to the lip. This face became much steeper in the time of Perabsen, as in 335 and 337. The bowls here, like those of Khosekhem in 339 to 346, are all deep. The facing of the edge became still more upright, as in 340, 341, and 342, and in the deepest bowls the lip is very thick and square, and much turned in, 343 to 346.

Pl. XXII, early iiird dynasty. This period is fully represented by the royal and princely tombs of Beyt Khallaf and Mahasneh, and other tombs of Reqaqneh. The comparisons therefore are well based, like those with the royal tombs of Abydos. Some of the steep lips remain, as 361 to 364 ; but in general the excessive lip had become so inconvenient that all lip was abandoned, and the brim reverted to the simple form of the early ist dynasty. The distinction from the earlier bowls is, however, in the round form of the inside. This began in the less careful work of Den, S.D. 81 ; and after the ist dynasty it is rarely that any internal corner was worked at the base. Thus the different ways of working the brim and the base pretty safely define the ages of bowls. At the end of the plate are a few forms, 365 to 371, for which no dated comparison is close enough, but they appear to belong to the less-known times of the iiird dynasty ; 365–6 may be Roman, as well as 972.

Pl. XXIII, iiird dynasty and onward. A tomb of the iiird dynasty at Gizeh gives parallels to these vases, 372 to 381. The style of flat dishes began to revive at 349 (since the old Hierakonpolis and Tarkhan examples, 198 to 203), and it appears here in 372, 373. The bowls, 374 to 379, are much like those of the iind and early iiird dynasties. The massive vase 380 probably turned outward to a brim ; perhaps with a wide mouth, as Beyt Khallaf xxvii, or a narrower mouth, as Gizeh vi E.

At the end of the iiird dynasty there is this very clumsy bowl from Meydum, 382. The recurved edges in 383 to 387 are like the pottery bowls from Meydum and elsewhere, apparently of the early ivth dynasty. This form is well adapted for pottery, to stiffen the brim, but is difficult to work in stone ; hence these probably originated from the pottery forms. Some at the base of the plate are undated, 388, 389 with peculiar flat brims, and 396. The conical vases in obsidian and basalt, 390 to 392, are from funerary sets of the vith dynasty (*Dendereh* xxi). The little flat-brim bowl, 395, has a scroll pattern on it, and is of the xiith dynasty from Kahun. The age of 393 and 394 is uncertain, but as 393 is of blue marble these are probably of the xiith dynasty ; the form occurs in the xviiith (*Ab.* III, xliv).

15. Pl. XXIV. *Spouted bowls.* The dated examples of open-spout bowls are of the reign of Den, and probably these, 397 to 403, should be assigned to that date, or rather later in the case of the rough work of 400 to 402. The smaller ones are beautifully made and of fine stones.

The double-spout bowl, 405, seems obviously related to the double-spout copper bowls of Khosekhemui; those probably were originated by the co-equal worship of Horus and Set at that time, neither of them greater nor less than the other, and to be adored simultaneously. The bowl is of fine thin work, but only in soft limestone. A single-spout bowl of limestone of the same form, 406, is probably of the same age.

The bowls with tubular spouts, 407, 408, are related to the tubular-spouted bowls of pottery made in the iiird to vith dynasties. As these stone bowls are of fine work they seem most like the delicate forms of the vth and vith dynasties, and a similar bowl is dated to the vith dynasty (*Dendereh* xxi). The deep small bowl, 409, of white marble, has a uraeus under the spout with its tail curling round the base. The style of this looks like that of the xiith dynasty. The little bowl, 410, is adapted from a fish form; as it is of gypsum, it is probably of the iind or iiird dynasty.

16. *Rimmed bowls.* This class appears to have been started at S.D. 80, about the reign of Zet, and it disappears after the iiird dynasty; thus it is characteristic of the first group of dynasties. The series is placed here in order of age, as shown by the fixed examples and the style of form. 411 to 415 are the taller and less specialised forms, and the others on to 424 are fixed to S.D. 80. From 425 to 436 they are of S.D. 81, or like those so dated. From 437 to 441 they are like those of S.D. 82 or the end of the ist dynasty. 442 to 444 appear to be late, by the coarse forms. 445 to 448 are like those of the iiird dynasty at Beyt Khallaf.

CHAPTER III

UPRIGHT VASES

17. Pl. XXV. *Barrel form.* The earlier forms leading to the barrel type are first given here. 449 is of the group figured in 12 and 211 to 219, and therefore probably from the tomb of Neit-hetep; the same outline, but of an oval plan, was found in that tomb (De Morgan, *Tombeau de Negadeh*, fig. 667). The forms 450–452, 455, 456 are like those of S.D. 80, and the tip of a vase 437 is from a tomb of that date. The less regular form, 453, may perhaps be an earlier stage, as it occurs in S.D. 77 and 78 (*Tarkhan* I, type 77d). The almost globular vase, 458, has the same form as the pottery (type 94l), dated to S.D. 79, 80. The succeeding forms, 459 to 461, are like those of S.D. 80; while the others, 462 to 475, are like those of S.D. 81. This type therefore was mainly of the middle of the ist dynasty, about the reign of Den. The method of sawing a cut to separate the brim from the body, as in 466, was started in that reign, as seen in *R.T.* II, type 282; and it lasted to the end of the iind dynasty, as in *Abydos* I, ix, 6, 7.

18. Pl. XXVI. *Squat form.* The barrel form which came to its maximum in S.D. 80, passed into the squat form which began in S.D. 81, the better formed and earlier examples, 478 to 490, being all of that age. The form was already greatly flattened, as in 485; and it became still flatter and more misshapen, as 491, 492, which are like those of the close of the iind dynasty. 495 is like the iiird dynasty type. The top was often inserted after the vase was hollowed, and it has been afterwards lost; hence the form 500. This seems to have led to a form without a mouth-piece, as 501, 502, which are so wide across the opening that they reach the form of bowls. A late development of this was with a tall neck, as 505, which is like a form of the ivth to vith dynasties (*Mahasna*, xxxv, 18). This class of vases is generally of gypsum in the end of the ist and in the iind dynasty; later, various grey and variegated marbles appear. The difficulty of hollowing so wide a vase with a narrow neck led to making it in two halves, as 480, 481. This method has been adopted by modern forgers, whose work in grey serpentine turned in a lathe is pretty well evident.

19. Pl. XXVII. *Collared form.* The top row, 506 to 517, is placed as introductory to this class, though some (such as 506) are almost nearer to 578, 579, and others. Half a dozen in this row can be dated by comparison, all to the vith dynasty. The length of the neck, or the pointed base, are the links with the collared forms, 518 to 532. Two unusual materials here are quartz crystal 509, and crystallized calcite 512. 509–512 have been hollowed by a tube drill only. The form with a double rim, 516, 517, seems to be the step leading to the collared form.

The collared vases, 518 to 527, are in no case datable outside of the vith dynasty. The example on a stand, 527, is much like a vase on stand which is certainly of the xviiith dynasty, 880; but the latter has only a plain neck, and not the double ridge, hence it is not of this class. Of course, pointed vases were always placed on ring stands, and so there is nothing surprising in such a combination being imitated at any period. The short forms, 528 to 532, were the degradation of the longer type, as is shown by the single-rim forms, 533 to 535, being still later. One, like 534, was found at Hu, grave 182, of rough work, and associated with so degraded a bowl form that it was assigned to about the ixth dynasty (*Diospolis*, xxviii).

20. *Peculiar types.* The use of shells for containing eye-paint dates from the iiird dynasty (see *Medum*, xxix, 17). In the vith dynasty, imitation shells carved in diorite were used (see *Dendereh*, xxi). The carved shells, here 536 to 538, probably belong to the xiith dynasty. 536 is of alabaster, 537 of slate, and 538 of blue paste ; the latter material was not used before the xiith dynasty.

The shallow rough dish, 539, is a model from the tomb of Qa, at the close of the ist dynasty.

The flat tray, 540, with lotus patterns incised, is most like the top of a stand of about the iiird dynasty. The rough style of decoration would agree well with this age, but there are no other examples for comparison.

The oblong stone dishes, 541, 542, are of sandstone and of alabaster. Such are dated to the xiith dynasty at Rifeh (*Gizeh and Rifeh*, xi A, 70) and at Hu (*Diospolis*, xxvii, W 38 ; xxx, Y 448). The little oblong alabaster dish, 543, is obviously connected with these, but no dated example has been found.

The upright pot of dark grey limestone, 544, is quite undated. The tube of blue marble, 545, is probably of the xiith dynasty ; it may be an early form of kohl tube. The solid form, 546, is well finished, except that the projecting foot is rough ; it looks as if it were a model lamp on stand, from a set of funerary models.

Bowls with figures of apes on the outside were made in the xiith dynasty, as in *Arabah*, ix, with two apes like fig. 547. This type was expanded in the xviith dynasty, with four apes, as in *Qurneh*, xxii, 9. The material is much the same in all these, a greyish marble, like the poorest examples of blue marble.

548 is a well-made vase of hard black steatite, with a thin lid, and a figure of an ape as a handle. Whether this is of the xiith or xviiith dynasty is uncertain. There is the same uncertainty in the date of the small oval vase, 549, with crocodiles on the edges of it.

21. Pl. XXVIII. *Vases of the vith to the xith dynasties.* After the vith dynasty, various degradations of type occurred, seen in the clumsy and rudely made forms attributable to that period. In all those from 550 to 604 there is not a single example of the blue marble which is characteristic of the xiith dynasty. There is a larger amount of limestones, plain and coloured, than in other ages, as 557, 563, 569, 595 of white, 573, 587, 588, 593 of buff, 572 of brown, and 604 of pink mixture.

From 550 to 582 they appear to be of the vith dynasty, with a few earlier. 553 is a rough solid model of limestone from the tomb of Qa (ist dyn.) ; from the same is 556 (solid). No. 552 is the first vase with a handle. Probably this and the succeeding vases, 557, 558, are from sets of vases for the seven ointments placed in the tomb ; see the complete set in *Riqqeh*, xiii, the table of thirty sets showing the forms and names, *R.*, xlix, and the statement *R.* 16. No. 559 may be a similar jug, broken ; it is from Hu, perhaps of the viith dynasty (*Diospolis*, xxviii). 552, 560, 561 are solid, and appear to be rough models of vases. The forms 562 to 568 are akin to those (508 to 512) which lead into the collared vases. 567 is solid, and was evidently one of the model vases on a slab of the vith dynasty, as in *Dendereh*, xxi. See also the similar forms in pottery of that age (*Dendereh*, xvi, 24, 25, 27).

The rounded forms 569 to 576 are merging toward the round-bottomed forms of the xiith dynasty 626 to 633, but the general type is like those from Mahasneh and Diospolis, of the vith dynasty. 576, which has a round bottom, is nevertheless before the xiith dynasty ; it is from a tomb at Mazghuneh with things of the vith dynasty style (*Mazghuneh*, p. 40, tomb A, pl. l, 3). 577 is much like the ist dynasty forms 451 and others ; it is distinguished from those by having a stronger lip and more fullness, like the vith dynasty forms from Zaraby (*Gizeh and Rifeh*, vii E, 118, 53). 578 is from Zaraby 118, just quoted. The fine forms of 579 to 582 are clearly of the vith dynasty ; 579 is from Zaraby, the flat wide brim of 580 is like the tips 93 and 95 of the vith, 581 and 582 are like the Mahasneh vases. The degradation of these forms is seen in the line 584 to 593 (some of which are dated to the xith dynasty); 584, 589, 590 from the Qurneh cemetery; and 588, compare with *Dendereh*, xx, 32 and 441. 593 has had a wider brim, which is now broken away. 595 is probably after the viiith dynasty, compared with those of Dendereh. 596 is from Qurneh, and so of the xith, as also are 597, 598 by comparison with the vase of Antef-aqer (*Dendereh*, xxii). The form of 599 is assigned to the xth dynasty at Rifeh and to the xiith at Hu; it was found with 600 and the scarab. 603, 604 are from Qurneh cemetery, and so of the xith dynasty.

22. Pl. XXIX. *Vases of the xiith dynasty.* The curiously flattened forms 605 to 607 are dated by one found at Hu (*Diospolis*, xxix, 348; xxx, 448) of the xiith dynasty. The more upright form, 607, is probably descended from the flat-bottomed vase in *Dendereh*, xxi, now in Cairo (18619). The form 608, 609 seems as if derived from the same, but there is no dated comparison for these, except a somewhat similar vase of Hatshepsut (Wilk. *M. and C.*, fig. 281). The whole class, 605 to 609, seems to be the source of the xviiith dynasty form 867 to 872. The little cups, 610 to 612, are dated by similar examples. The very small vases, 613 to 621, are connected with the dwarf pottery of the xith dynasty (*Qurneh*, xvi, 263–282); from the good forms, and being mostly of blue marble, these appear to be of the xiith. 625 is of blue and black glaze; it is entered here for comparison with 612.

The round-bottomed vases, almost globular, seem to belong entirely to the xiith dynasty, and 626 must be so classed by the form, though none as large have been found dated. The insertion of the neck separately is like 629. Nos. 627, 629, and 632 are all made in two halves and joined. 633 is dated to the xiith by *Abydos* III, xi, 26. The fashion of the petalled mouth 635 to 637 is dated by such a vase found in an untouched burial with a scarab of the xiith dynasty (Peet, *Cem. Abyd.* II, xiii, 9, 10); other objects of the xiith and xviiith dynasties were found in plundered burials above this, but must not be confused with the earlier things. In 635 the neck is inserted in the body at the shoulder; it has a stopper of alabaster, stuck tight at present. The outside is highly polished, as was usual in this age. 636 is a similar neck, for insertion in a vase. The two pieces 638, 639 are undated. 640 to 642 are solid models of vases; they have shallow holes on opposite sides, and the largest one has a groove in the neck above the holes. These holes were probably for inserting a spout and handle to each model, perhaps made of copper wire. No. 643 is a clumsy kohl pot of black limestone, from Harageh and therefore of the xiith dynasty, though nothing else was found with it. 644, 645 are solid models of vases with sealing caps upon them. 646 is a finely made form which had loop handles on each side, and probably a brim, now lost. 647 is the *khnum* vase, with a square lug in front for lifting it; this is the more classical form of the type 557–559. A type peculiar to this period is 648–649, with a flat base and wide conical brim; these examples are from the xiith dynasty cemeteries of Rifeh and Harageh.

The vith dynasty type 579 to 582 was continued in the xiith, as in 650 to 654. A change is seen in the conical brim of 652, like that of the kohl pots below; 653 seems to be a funeral model, with only a slight hollowing.

The forms with fully rounded base are very usual in pottery of the xiith dynasty, and are also characteristic of the stone vases. The globular form, 626–632, is noted above; but the drop form, 655–659, is the more marked in the pottery. In stone it has sometimes two, three, or four bands on the brim; one of these found in the royal burials of Dahshur fixes it to the xiith dynasty, agreeing thus with others from Hu, Rifeh, and Harageh.

The kohl pots 661–663 are of unusual size, larger than any of the examples of the xiith dynasty on the next plate. 666 is a pottery copy of stone form, perhaps to imitate serpentine, being reddish brown with a smooth surface; such imitations were made at this age, as the black pottery 124, imitating black serpentine.

CHAPTER IV

KOHL POTS

23. Pl. XXX. The series of kohl pots was drawn by Prof. Hamada of Kyoto University, in January 1915, as he kindly wished to do a piece of systematic work while in England during his archaeological travels. It seemed better not to alter his drawings by filling in a ground, as the outer side of his lines is the true outline. For the sake of completing the subject he drew also the kohl tubes, which are mainly of wood and ivory. These are published by photograph in the catalogue of *Objects of Daily Use*, and therefore without sections. As they are small objects, and some with detail, they are here printed on a scale of one half, not one-third like the other stone vases.

As the greater part of the kohl pots are of the Middle Kingdom, and hardly any dated precisely to a dynasty, it is best to class them entirely by form. The divisions here followed are :

679–682. *Necked forms.*

683–685. *Handled forms.*

686–697. *Vase on stand,* also of xviiith dynasty.

698–713. *Thin brim,* also of xviiith dynasty.

714–728. *Thick conical brim.* All the above are of the Middle Kingdom.

729–746. xviiith dynasty forms, with *high shoulder.*

Pl. XXXI. The necked forms are probably the earliest, about the beginning of the xiith dynasty, as they link on to the xith dynasty forms 584–593. The handled forms have no immediate forerunners, but seem as if they had descended by some unknown line from the early dynastic vases, like 163 to 167. As they are all three of blue marble, they are almost certainly of the xiith dynasty.

The vases on stands are made sometimes separate from the stand, but more usually in one block. They are mostly with the thin brim but also extend to the conical brim class. They are rare in proportion to the other classes, the number here being due to my selecting them as peculiar, while the common forms were seldom purchased.

The thin-brim vases have the early egg form 698–701, like the necked vase 679. They pass on to the later angular shoulder form, as 713. 706 is classed here by the type, but it was found on Heqreshu knoll at Abydos, and by this locality it would be of the xviiith dynasty. 708 was picked up by me at Kahun, with the original linen tied over the mouth of it.

The deep conical brim is presumably the nearest to the xviiith dynasty, as it was usual at that time. But it is here of the xiith dynasty from Rifeh, 724, and three of them are of blue marble. The type often appears among the xiith dynasty burials.

The high, and often angular, shoulder is the mark of the xviiith dynasty, as seen in *Gizeh and Rifeh,* xxvii A. None of these are of blue marble, and they are mostly of awkward and badly proportioned shapes, which ignore the original idea of the type, such as 679, 700, or 714.

24. *Kohl tubes.* The kohl pot died out and was superseded by the kohl tube. This change took place during the long reign of Tehutmes III. I have not found a publication of any kohl pot dated later than Tehutmes III. In one tomb, *Arabah* 276, which has scarabs of Tehutmes III and Amenhetep II, there were two much-chipped kohl pots, evidently long used before burial. This is the latest fixed date ; there were none at Gurob, which site began under Tehutmes III ; there were none in the tomb of Tehutmes IV, nor in that of Yuaa. The beginning of the tube is seen in tombs *Arabah* 155 and 294, both associated with the kohl pot, and dated to Tehutmes III. In the Maket tomb, under Tehutmes III, there were four pots (one with a figure, one with a stand), and one palm-capital tube (*Illahun,* xxvii). In the tomb of Tehutmes IV were many kohl tubes (misnamed as pots in publication), of the palm-capital form. In groups dated to Amenhetep III, Tutankhamen, and Ramessu II there are tubes but never pots (Gurob). At Tell el Amarna there were many tubes but no pots. The change must have been rather sudden, apparently within a generation. The pots of limestone, blackened, with yellow incised patterns as 745, 746, are the later stage, being dated to Hatshepsut (*Arabah,* xxi, 155) and Tehutmes III (*El Amrah,* li, D 59). They are an imitation of ebony inlaid with gold. The tube is due to Syrian-Semitic influence (see the name of Job's daughter Keren-ha-puk, " horn of paint").

Of the kohl tubes there are some additional examples in the catalogue of *Objects of Daily Use,* pl. xxii, figs. 1, 2, lid and pot engraved ; figs. 3, 4, 5, apes and seated woman holding a tube ; figs. 15 grey serpentine sextuple tubes, 16 wood quadruple tubes, 17 blue glazed quintuple tubes, 20 wood single tubes, 23 palm capital tube of wood, 24 bone tube, 25, 26 wooden tubes, 31 to 36 reed tubes, 37, 38 Roman and Coptic wooden tubes.

Fig. 748 is a limestone block with cursive hieroglyphic inscriptions of the " Divine father, priest of Ptah, cleanser of the temple of Memphis, AUFHENSI, chief engraver." On the other side is a figure of a falcon wearing the crown of Lower Egypt. This is probably about the xxist dynasty. The use of several tubes together was to hold the various colours and medicaments for the eyes. Those figured here are of serpentine, alabaster, and four of wood. The ape (755) holding a tube with a figure of Taurt on the front (shown below) is of browned limestone ; it is duplicated after 807 here. The bone tubes carved as columns, 756 to 761, are of the xviiith dynasty ; see a pair on a stand in *El Amrah,* xlvii, 115. They are of interest in the study of architecture. Following them are wooden tubes with cross-line patterns. The double tube, 765, is of ivory. The triple tube, 766, is of wood ; it has a similar figure of an ibex on the other side. The three compound tubes, 767–769, are of steatite, probably Roman. The last has the figure of Harpocrates standing in a shrine, guarded by couchant lions; there is also a lion at the foot of the tube.

My best thanks are due to Prof. Hamada for assisting the catalogue with this series of drawings.

CHAPTER V

VASES OF THE XVIIITH DYNASTY

25. Pl. XXXII. *Cups.* A few of these may belong to the next dynasty, and one such (785) has been placed here, as it compares with others which are earlier. 770 is a fragment of a great bowl of grey serpentine, which was fully 18 ins. in diameter, bearing the titles and name of Tehutmes III. The fish bowl, 771, is the original form of the little rough fish bowls met with later (886 and *Illahun*, xvii, 41). The bowl 772, with four handles, is probably derived from the earlier type of the bowl with four rams' heads (*Kahun*, viii, 3). The slate bowl, 773, has groups of fishes and lotus incised on the inside. The date of it is uncertain, but probably of the xviiith dynasty. The slight handle carved on some bowls, as 771, 774, 785, 787–789, is shown above it in plan; it is derived from the projection which is riveted on to metal bowls to carry a loop for suspension, as in the metal bowls 39, 40. Another bowl with decoration is 794, with fish and lotus pattern; this is certainly of the xviiith or xixth dynasty, by the style. A rather shallower bowl than 786 was used in the vith–viiith dynasties (*Dendereh*, xx, 242).

The set of funerary models, 799–806, was found in the knoll where offerings were deposited at Abydos in the xviiith dynasty. They are closely like those deposited as offerings to Aohmes I (*Abydos* III, xlvi). Some unusual pieces, 807 to 812, probably belong to this dynasty. 807 is a fragment of a cylindrical alabaster jar with an incised pattern of sepals, and of buds on long stems; no jar of this form is known after the early dynasties, but this work clearly seems much later. 755 is given under that number before. 808 is a steatite figure of Taurt, drilled down from the head for a kohl tube. 809 is a bird dish, and 810 another with a flying bird; no exact parallel for these is dated. 811 seems to be a degradation of an animal bowl; one edge is broken away. 812 is a little vase with a monkey holding it and a baboon before it.

The lotus cup was a very favourite design of the New Kingdom. The first one here, 813, is so closely the form of a pottery cup of the ixth–xth dynasties (*Gizeh and Rifeh*, xiii A, 3, and see *Mochlos*, ix, M 12) that it seems difficult not to accept that date for it. Yet there is no lotus chalice dated before the xviiith dynasty. If 813 is early it may carry with it 816, 817; but the work of all these seems to be like that of the other lotus cups. Possibly the form was conserved in some other land, and introduced in the ixth and again in the xviiith dynasty. Lotus cups sometimes have the petals in relief, as on a fragment, 804, 818, from Tell el Amarna, the base of which is broken away. Other such cups of Amenhetep III were found in Sinai (*Researches*, fig. 145).

26. Pl. XXXIII. *Tazze.* The tazza with upright sides is peculiar to the xviiith dynasty, and does not seem to have any prototype in Egypt. It was a favourite form in Palestine, and it may be a Syrian fashion imported; the corrugated form strongly suggests a derivation from hammered metal-work. The evidence of dating shows the plainer form to be earlier than that with the middle band. The plain form, as 825–826, occurs in the Maket tomb, of the same date of Tehutmes III at Abydos (*Cem. Ab.* III, x, 6), and 829 from Tell el Amarna. The middle rib occurs from the tomb of Sadiamia at Gurob, about Tehutmes IV (*Kahun*, 35, xviii, 6), and under Amenhetep III (*Illahun*, xvii, 10), and Ramessu II (*Ill.*, xviii, 23). Thus the overlap of the two-ribbed and three-ribbed forms seems to have been during the time of Amenhetep III. The four-ribbed form, 837, is coarsely made, and apparently the latest, bordering on the style of the corrugated bronze buckets of Europe. The earlier two-ribbed forms have little or no foot; a distinct foot is found in the later two-ribbed 829; and a separate foot was made for some three-ribbed bowls, 832, 833, which only have a slight peg for attachment. The foot of 832 is not known to belong to it, but as it fits so closely, and is in accordance with one in Cairo (18218), we may fairly associate the two pieces.

27. *Tubular forms.* The tubular vase descends from the pottery of the xiith dynasty, see *Hyksos Cities*, x, and *Gizeh and Rifeh*, xxv, xxvi, xxvii D, H, K. It was one of the commonest forms of pottery, especially in the early part of the xviiith dynasty, and decorated in the later part. It was not so usual in alabaster, but yet fairly common. 838 to 842 are probably all of the xviiith dynasty, and the wreath incised on the last is like that on a piece of a vase of Horemheb in the Cairo Museum (18790). 840 from the rather clumsy outline might be supposed later, but it is finely polished and therefore not likely to be Ramesside. The very thin translucent alabaster, 843, is of a pottery form very usual about the middle of the xviiith dynasty, and is most closely paralleled by pots of Tehutmes III (Maket, *Illahun*, xxvii, 42) and of Amenhetep II (*Six Temples*, v, 1). 844 is from Rifeh, of late xviiith dynasty (*G.R.*, xxvii A, 257). The bowl, 845, is of about Tehutmes III, see *Riqqeh*, xiv, 61, grave 601.

28. *High-necked vases.* The series of high-necked vases, 846 to 859, seems to have had a brief career; I have not observed, after one of Hatshepsut (*Rifeh*, xxvii H, 206), any example dated outside of the reign of Tehutmes III. In that reign there were five in the Maket tomb, and another of that age from Abydos. The type seems to have passed at that time into the large form with handles, 883 (Cairo, 18734), which continued to the end of the dynasty, 885 (Cairo, 18790). An indication that the type did not continue long after Tehutmes III is seen in the clumsy and debased form, 854 being the origin of the type 860, which in turn set the fashion of pottery at the close of the dynasty (*Illahun*, xvii, 5; xx, 13). The latest debasement of this type is dated to Ramessu II, in 909.

29. Pl. XXXIV. The *handled vases*, 862, 863, are not dated closely, but are clearly of about the mid-xviiith dynasty; as also probably 864, which is carved in one piece for the body and bird, with a neck set in and joined to the bird's beak.

The vases with three handles are probably foreign, perhaps Cretan, in idea; in fact, handles in general are due in Egypt to foreign influence. They are of two types: (A) at the neck two handles opposite, and a third at right angles as 865, and a glass vase of late xviiith dynasty from Gurob (*Illahun*, xx, 11); (B) three handles equidistant on the shoulder, as 866, also in pottery of Ramessu II (*Ill.*, xviii, 51), of Sety II (*Ill.*, xix, 11), and in Crete (*Ann. Brit. Sch., Athens*, vii, 91; xi, 14, and others). The stone and the work of 866 is not like any Egyptian vase that I know, and it may well be a Cretan importation.

30. *Pear-shaped vases.* The pear-shaped type, 867–872, is well dated. 869 is like one of Maket, 868 has a figure-handle, like a Maket kohl pot, 867 has the name of Amenhetep III, 872 is like one from Gurob dated to Amenhetep III (*Ill.*, xvii, 6), and 869 is like the funerary vases of Yuaa. Hence from Tehutmes III to Amenhetep III is the range. The small forms 873 to 876 are not dated, and are only tentatively placed here. 877 is from Rifeh of the xviiith dynasty; it is the ancestor of a form of the xxvith dynasty (Cairo, 18489). 878 contains brown ointment, so the inner form is unknown; it has a peg below to fit into a stand, which is only suggested here. This, and 879, are clearly dated by pottery types, to the last half of the xviiith dynasty. 880 is from tomb 78 Meydum, certainly of the xviiith. 881, 882 are probably of the same age, but not dated by comparisons.

The great jars with loop handles are dated to Tehutmes III (as 883, Cairo, 18734) and to Tutankh-amen 885. They were often imitated in pottery about the latter time. 883 contains brown oint-ment, like 869.

CHAPTER VI

VASES OF LATE PERIODS

Vases of the Ramessides and Bubastites

31. Pl. XXXV. *Saucers.* In most cases these are not well fixed in date, but are presumably of this period, by their deterioration from the previous types. The series of the bird dishes, 887–893, begins in the last dynasty, but these are very degraded copies. 887 has the tail roughly painted. 888 has a goose-head handle projecting. 889 has apparently a bird head at the opposite end. 890–891 seem to be copied from the trussed-goose dishes of the last dynasty, which originated in the xiith dynasty, as known at Lisht and Hawara pyramids. 892 has traces of the limbs, and a straight-tail handle, while 893 retains only the handle. Lastly the handle became a lotus flower, retaining traces of the limbs, 895, or with the flower alone, 894. 896 has a row of triangles incised around the brim, and filled in with black. 897 looks like a clumsy copy of 821; or it might be the foot of an early table-stand, like 148 but inverted. 908 has a gold binding to the lid, a gold hinge and band round the pot, and a gold loop and pin in front fastening into a silver socket. The powdery black state of the silver proves the an-tiquity of it. The pot above, 907, has had a swivel lid. Of the large jar of Ramessu II, 909, there is only a portion, but enough to show the form as here drawn, which is a very debased copy of 854. 910 and 911 are debasements of the type 846 to 859, and probably a dynasty later than those. 912 is interesting as a type quite unknown in Egypt but favoured in Crete. This form of lid occurs in Knossos, Mid Minoan I period (*Ann. Brit. Sch., Athens*, ix, 95) ; and of Mid or Late Minoan, found by Seager (*Mochlos*, pp. 88, 89 ; IX, iiia). This is probably therefore of Cretan origin.

32. Pl. XXXVI. *Pilgrim bottles.* The pilgrim bottle type is foreign to Egypt, but was brought in under Tehutmes III, or perhaps earlier, probably from Cyprus. At that time it was shorter in the neck than 915 ; see Maket tomb, Amenhetep III and Tutankhamen groups in *Illahun*, xxvii, 4 ; xvii, 21, 42 ; and under Akhenaten, in Apiy tomb, *Riqqeh*, xvi, 2. The body and the neck were lengthened in the xixth dynasty, as under Ramessu II, 917 and 919, like that of Sety II (*Illahun*, xxi, 25). The vase 917 is a very rare example of a dated vase, with names of Ramessu II and Queen Nefertari, mounted in gold. The brim, outsides of the handles, and edge of the body are covered with gold strips cast to fit, and a band of beaten gold crosses the shoulder. The age of this mounting is guaranteed by the gold passing a conical foot of sheet silver, which is clearly corroded anciently. 916 has a very narrow neck, so that it cannot be measured inside ; but it is doubtless well hollowed, as the body is made in two halves, joined together on one side close to the edge. 918 is from Gurob, and has a loop of soft cord through the handles. 920 is a circular jug, of the same style of stone and work as 919.

33. *Tub pots.* The various tub pots, widest at the base, 922, 923, 926–928, are all undated. There can be little doubt from the style that they are late Ramesside or Bubastite, but neither from excavations nor museums is there any fixed age. The only dating point is that one occurs in a North Syrian cemetery, which brings it to 700 B.C. or later (*Ancient Egypt*, 1917, 41). Looking at the forms of stone vases from Libya, in *Anc. Eg.*, 1915, 163, 167, it seems that the origin of these wide-based pots was an influence from the West. 924 is obviously copied from the usual pottery form of about the xxiiird dynasty, such as *Qurneh*, l, 795. A similar character is seen in a Ramesside vase from Gurob (see *Illahun*, xix, 42).

Some forms of uncertain age are in the lower half of pl. xxxvi. 931 is made of nummulitic limestone hardened by infiltration. As large vases of this form have not been discovered, this was set aside as suspect. It does not, however, appear to have any trace of modern work, and the inside has been hollowed out at first by a large tube drill hole, 2 ins. wide. Such a drill has not been used since the Old Kingdom, so far as I have seen ; I should therefore credit this vase to the vith dynasty, resembling 514, 515, and *Mahasna*, xxxvi, 23. The black steatite bowl 932 might be of the Old Kingdom, but the soft material is probably late. The very squat type 933 is probably of the xxiiird or xxvth dynasty (see *Hyksos Cities*, xix, 85). The group 936–938 is early Ptolemaic (see *Anthedon*). The great basalt tub 940 looks akin to the tub pots 922, 923, 926–928. 939 is hollowed from the bottom, and closed by a flat plate ; there is no parallel to this form.

Vases of Saitic and Ptolemaic Age

34. Pl. XXXVII. *Alabastra.* There is a remarkable absence of stone vases after the Ramesside times, and, barring a very few large jars, there is nothing of Saite age except the alabastra. 941–942 are perhaps of xxvth dynasty, 941 being from Abusir el Melek, sold along with the scarab of the late vizier Nekht (*Scarabs*, lvii, C). There is only a presumption from the forms of 943–946, to place them at this age.

947 is a well-known type of pottery of about the xxiind–xxiiird dynasties. It was derived from the large egg-shaped jars with handles, of the xviiith dynasty, and in turn it originated the series of alabastra 948 to 971, coming down to the Roman age. The form of handle in 948–949, the plan of which is placed here above the side, was evidently made for tying down a lid over the pot, to hold the string in the notch. Very few of the alabastra are recorded of fixed period. Some at Yehudiyeh, like 955, 956, are at the beginning of the xxvith dynasty or rather earlier, shown by the mirror with them not yet being circular, as in the xxvith. The fibula, which was found with another vase like 963, is also early xxvith (*Hyksos Cities*, xxA).

The large vases 958, 959 are two of a group of four, which were thoroughly broken up and buried in a pit in the palace of Apries at Memphis. This intentional destruction is probably to be dated to the Persian invasion, in 525 B.C. : hence the vases may be dated to the reign of Apries or Amasis. The other two vases are larger, and of the forms 949 and 958 (*Memphis* II, xvi).

The form 982 in gypsum is usual in early Greek tombs, of the xxvith dynasty and onward.

In later times a sharp shoulder and tubular neck were adopted, 966–968, apparently in imitation of vases with a separately cut neck and mouth inserted, though these here are all in one piece. 966 and 967 are very thin and translucent. 968 is like a vase dated to Necho, in the British Museum (Wilk., 275, 3). 969 was found with a gold necklace and a ring of the 1st century A.D., at Kafr Ammar (*Heliopolis*, xxxix, 20–24). A vase similar to 969 was found at Kafr Ammar, inscribed in Greek *Paraiguptou A . . rakinon*, which may be restored as *Anthrakinon*. Theophrastus describes the anthrax as being brought from Egypt, near the cataracts and Syene, and Pliny refers to the Ethiopian carbuncle. It seems then that this alabastron was intended for the exportation of garnets. The lettering appears to be Ptolemaic (*Heliopolis and Kafr Ammar*, xxxvii). The long tubular neck of 970–971 is dated by the latter being found in a group at Mazghuneh (*Labyrinth*, xlvi), which by its general style belongs to the 1st century A.D. This seems to be the close of this type, as no trace of it was found in the large cemetery of Hawara of the 1st century onwards.

35. Pl. XXXVIII. *Vases of Roman age.* Dishes with two or four lugs are often found in Roman remains, such as 972, 977. The flat alabaster dish 973 is of the 1st century from Mazghuneh, 974 is the simplest form of the toilet saucers, which were later decorated with relief figures; these are fully described in the catalogue of *Objects of Daily Use*, both the 9 examples at the College and 19 elsewhere. This earliest form has a spout which is partly open, but pierced at the end; the inside is plain turned, without decoration, the outside has a plaited pattern. 975 is part of a dish, having a raised brim with wreath pattern, and a band of criss-cross pattern on the flat bottom. 976 is a gypsum bowl with very rude lug handles; the age is quite uncertain. No. 979 is a clumsy bowl of black granite.

The use of mortars for pounding was at least as early as the xviiith dynasty; two were in groups D 115, 119, and *Amrah and Abydos*, xlvii, xlviii. The regularly formed mortars seem to begin with the Greek influence in the xxvith dynasty, see one of Psamtek II in Cairo (18736); the handles in this are deep, and cut square below, as 981. The mortar of Nekhtnebef has shallow handles, cut square (*Abydos* I, lxx, 11). That from the deposits of Ptolemy II has deep handles, cut sloping below, as 982 (*Naukratis* I, xxvi). It may seem that the handle is a guide to the date. 983 has grooves cut in the handles, as shown at the side, implying that a lid was tied down over it.

A unique dish, 984, has a deeply incised figure of a falcon on the inside. The outside pattern is also without a parallel, but from the work it is doubtless of the 1st or 2nd century A.D. The other bowls, 985–991, have no fixed comparison elsewhere, but appear to be all Roman.

The alabaster vases with a ring on the neck, 993–995, are of the 1st century A.D., by 993 found at Mazghuneh. This place also dates 992. The tub pot 996, of steatite with loop handles, hardly seems to be of the Ramesside family, but is probably later. 997 is a flat slab with sunk compartments, and a hole for a pivoting lid; it was probably for ointments or colours.

CATALOGUE OF STONE VASES

In the following list, the first numbers are those on the black and white plates. The material is stated next; colours are marked as bk. black, bl. blue, gn. green, gy. grey, wt. white; names specially used for materials are *alabaster* for veined crystalline carbonate of lime, *marble* if massive, *limestone* if opaque, *gypsum* for sulphate of lime, *dolomite* for carbonate of lime and magnesia.

The numbers in [ ] refer to the photographs on pls. i to v.

The sign = shows that the vase here is that found at the place named, or published in the reference following. A reference without = is for comparison of a similar specimen which is dated. The Arabic numbers 77 to 82 refer to Sequence Dates of the early dynasties; the Roman numbers are those of dynasties. Type numbers refer to the types published with dates in *Tarkhan* I, pls. xxxii–xliv, and *Tarkhan* II, pls. xxv–xxvii.

The publications, or tombs, referred to here are: A.A., *El Amrah and Abydos*; Ab. I, II, III, *Abydos* I, II, III; A. C. W., *Abydos* III; Barnasht, see *Labyrinth*, 37; B., Ballas in *Naqada*; Cem. Ab., *Cemeteries of Abydos* I, II, III; D., *Dendereh*; D.P., *Diospolis Parva*; F.T., *Fayum Towns* (Grenfell); G.A., Garstang, *Arabah*; G.R., *Gizeh and Rifeh*; G.T., Garstang, *Third Egyptian Dynasty*; H., *Hyksos and Israelite Cities*; Il., *Illahun*; K., *Kahun*; L. or L.G., *Labyrinth, Gerzeh and Mazghuneh*; M.K., *Mahasna and Bet Khallaf*; M.M., *Meydum and Memphis* III; N., *Naqada*; N.N., no number; P.E.,

Prehistoric Egypt; P.T., *Tarkhan*; P.G., *Gaza*; Q., Quibell, generally *El Kab*; R. or R.M., *Riqqeh and Memphis* VI; R.K., Reisner *Kerma* (*Mus. Fine Arts Bull.*, 1915, Dec.); R.T., *Royal Tombs* II, pls. xlvi–liii G; T.R., *Tombeau Royal de Negadeh* (De Morgan); *Wilk.* Wilkinson, *Manners and Customs*; Z., *Zaraby* in G.R.

Plate VI.

1. Gy. limestone = P.T. 315 . . . . s.d. 77
2. Alabaster banded [21].
3. ,, ... type 50 l s.d. 78
4. ,, = P.T. 1023, & 36 . s.d. 78
5. ,, = ,, 1023 . . s.d. 78
6. ,, = ,, 261 King Ka s.d. 78
7. ,, = ,, 414 Narmer s.d. 78
8. ,, = ,, 10 . . s.d. 79
9. ,, { bulging sides type 51 p s.d. 78
   R.T. 362 s.d. 79
   wide wave R.T. 348 s.d. 79 }
10. ,, top, see R.T. 361 s.d. 79
11. ,, = P.T. 111 . . s.d. 79
12. Basalt [3] (Neit-hetep) R.T. 357, 360 . s.d. 79
13. Bl. volcanic ash R.T. 190 . . s.d. 79
14. Alabaster = P.T. 1523 . . . . . s.d. 79
15. ,, ... type 61 j, l s.d. 80

Plate VII.

16. Alabaster form. G.R. v A, 8; top Ab. I, xlvi, 26 s.d. 80
17. ,, ... G.R. v A, 10, 19 s.d. 80
18. Gy. volcanic ash. R.T. 364 . type 54 r s.d. 80
19. Alabaster . . . . . type 54 v s.d. 80
20. ,, = G.R. Zet, 11 . . . . s.d. 80
21. ,, [30] G.R. v B, 31 . type 54 p s.d. 80
22. ,, ... type 54 v s.d. 80
23. ,, ... Ab. I, xliii, 60 s.d. 80
24. ,, ... type 61 l s.d. 80
25. ,, ... type 61 l s.d. 80
26. ,, ... Ab. I, xlvi, 7. s.d. 80
27. Bk. basalt . . . . . R.T. 81 . s.d. 81
28. Alabaster . . . type 54 n s.d. 80, 81
29. Bk. steatite . . . . . R.T. 375 s.d. 81
30. Alabaster . . . . . type 54 f s.d. 81

Plate VIII.

31. Slate . . . type 54 n s.d. 80, 81
32. Alabaster . . type 54 w, 55 c s.d. 80, 81
33. ,, = P.T. 165 . . . . . s.d. 81
34. Gypsum . . . . type 54 t s.d. 81
35. Alabaster . . . type 54 l, 62 w s.d. 81
36. ,, ... type 63 m s.d. 81
37. Gypsum [16] . . . type 62 w s.d. 81
38. Alabaster [17] = P.T. 165 . . . s.d. 81
39. Alabaster . . . . type 63 m s.d. 81
40. ,, ... R.T. 339, 374 s.d. 81
41. ,, ... type 62 p s.d. 81
42. ,, ... type 62 w s.d. 81
43. ,, ... type 62 w s.d. 81

Plate IX.

44. Gypsum . . . R.T. 338, 339 s.d. 81
45. Alabaster . . . . type 62 e s.d. 81
46. ,, = P.T. 165 . . . . . s.d. 81
47. ,, = ,, 107 . . . . . s.d. 81
48. ,, = Q. . . . type 62 r s.d. 81
49. ,, ... type 62 w s.d. 81
50. ,, = Q. 711 . . type 62 g s.d. 81
51. ,, = Q. 62 . type 62 c s.d. 80, 81
52. Gypsum = P.T. 191 . . . . . s.d. 81
53. Alabaster = Q. 177 . . type 62 b (?) s.d. 81
54. ,, = Q. . . . type 62 b, k s.d. 81
55. ,, = Q. . . . type 62 e s.d. 81
56. ,, = Q. 158 . . type 62 k s.d. 81
57. Gypsum . . . . type 62 e s.d. 81
58. Alabaster = Q.M. . . type 62 k s.d. 81
59. ,, = Q. 867 . . type 62 w s.d. 81
60. Gypsum = P.T. 231 . . . . . s.d. 81
61. Alabaster . . ? later than 62 l s.d. 81

Plate X.

62. Limestone, solid = Qa tomb . . . . s.d. 82
63. Alabaster . . . . type 63 m s.d. 81
64. ,, = P.T. 231 . . . . . s.d. 81
65. ,, G.R. vi B, 94 . . II
66. ,, Ab. I, x, 35 (?) . end II
67. ,, = Q. 311, M.K. xxii, 3, 12 . early III
68. ,, Ab. I, x, 30 . . end II
69. ,, M.K. xxii, 11 . . early III
70. ,, M.K. xi . . ,, III
71. ,, M.K. xxii, 9 . . ,, III
72. ,, M.K. xi, xxiv . . ,, III
73. ,, = Q. 233, M.K. xxii, 11 . . ,, III
74. ,, [23] = Q. Mastaba, M.K. xxii, 10 . ,, III
75. ,, = Q. 526, M.K. xxii, 8, 9 . ,, III
76. Gypsum [22] M.K. xxii, 9 . . ,, III

Plate XI.

77. Alabaster [34].
78. ,, banded.
79. ,,
80. ,, [24] . . Ab. II, xiv, 289 V
81. ,, [25] . . Ab. II, xiv, 290 ? V
82. ,, = Zaraby VI
83. ,, { G.R. vii E, Zaraby 3, 5 } VI
84. ,, [26]
85. ,, [27] M.K. xxxvi, 5
86. ,, [28]

87. Alabaster [35]. G.R. vii E, 5 . . VI
88. Limestone [29].
89. Alabaster [36].
90. Basalt [37].
91. Alabaster [38] M.K. xxxvi, 2 . . . VI
92. ,,
93A. ,, of Khufu [ii A] . . . IV
93B.C. ,, of Teta and Pepy I [48] [ii A] . VI
94. Bl. marble as Pepy II Ab. II, xxi, 7 . VI
95. Diorite [49] M.K. xxxviii, 13. VI
96. Syenite. VI
97. Alabaster [40] D. xx, 480 . . . IX–XI
98. ,, [41] D.P. xxviii, Y 250 . X
99. ,, [42] G.R. 194 . . . X
100. ,,
101. ,, = Rifeh 215, G.R. xi A . ? XI
102. ,, [50] D. xxii, Antefaqer . XI
103. ,, D.P. xxviii, Y 250 . X
104. ,, Cairo 18107, Emsaht . ? XI

PLATE XII.
105. Gy. wt. marble.
106. Br. bk. serpentine [43] G.R. xi A, 215 . XII
107. Alabaster D.P. xxix, W 72 XII
108. ,, ,, W 32 XII
109. ,, [51] ,, Y 372 XII
110. Bl. paste.
111. Pink-gy. marble.
112. Alabaster.
113. Bk. serpentine.
114. Bl. marble = Kahun Il. xiii, 1 . . XII
115. Br. bk. serpentine [45].
116. Gy. bk. serpentine. Cem. Ab. III, viii, 12 ? XII
117. Bk. serpentine.
118. Alabaster [44].
119. ,, [46] = Kahun viii, 29, no lid . XII
120. Bk. serpentine = D.P. xxix, Y 372 . XII
121. Alabaster [47] R.K., vert. edge . . XII
122. ,,
123. ,,
124. Bk. pottery.
125. Alabaster [53].
126. Br. serpentine [52].
127. Dark bl. paste.
128. Gy. marble [156], as 129, Ab. III, xliv . XII
129. Alabaster = Kahun (cf. *K.* xii, 12) . XII
130. ,,
131. Limestone.
132. Alabaster [157] Gizeh, G.R. xi A . . XII
133. ,, Deir el Bahri, Hatshepsut.
134. ,, ,, ,,
135. ,, Amu, Tehutmes III.
136. ,, Nubt, ,,
137. ,, Koptos ,,
138. ,, ,, ,,
139. Alabaster G.A. xvii, Nekheb, Amenhetep II.
140. ,, Busasu fish, place ? ,,
141. ,, Thinis ,,
142. ,, Thebes, temple of ,,

PLATE XIV.
143. Slate [73].
144. Basalt, stand . . . . . . end III
145. Gy. volcanic ash, stand.
146. Limestone.
147. Alabaster G.T. viii III
148. ,, = P.T. 250 . . . . . S.D. 81
149. Diorite G.T. viii III
150. Alabaster ,,
151. ,, [116] ,,
152. Diorite ,,
153. Buff limestone ,,

PLATE XV.
154. Bk. and wt. porphyry [62] R.T. 72 . S.D. 81
155. [65] R.T. 130 . S.D. 82
156. Alabaster [55] = Tarkhan 19 . . S.D. 79
157. Bk. and wt. porphyry [64] M.K. xxiv . III
158. Alabaster = Tarkhan 61 . . . S.D. 81
159. Pink marble [55] . . . R.T. 72 S.D. 81
160. Bl. marble . . . . ? XII
161. Alabaster = Harageh XII
162. Bk. wt. porphyry [63] see R.T. 127 . ? S.D. 81
163. Buff limestone [122] G.T. xii, 38 . . III
164. Alabaster [138] ,, . . III
165. Bk. wt. marble by stone . . III
166. Alabaster [124] = Tarkhan 100 . . S.D. 81
167. ,,
168. Bk. and wt. porphyry [66] G.T. vii . III
169. Alabaster Naqada ix, 51 . . ? S.D. 75
170. ,, [125] ,, . . ? S.D. 75
171. ,, [126] ,, ix, 47 . . ? S.D. 75
172. ,, [127] . . . type 71 f S.D. 77
173. ,, [128] . . . type 71 y S.D. 77
174. ,, cut down.
175. ,, [129] . . . type 71 j S.D. 78
176. ,, [130] Naqada, ix, 51 . . ? S.D. 75
177. ,, = P.T. 1801 . . . . S.D. 78
178. ,, = Zaraby 83 VI

PLATE XVI.
179. Alabaster = P.T. 1023 . . . . S.D. 78
180. ,, = Hierakonpolis . R.T. 297 S.D. 79
181. Bk. steatite.
182. Alabaster = P.T. 20 . . . . S.D. 78
183. ,, = ,, 414 . . . . S.D. 78
184. ,, = ,, ,, ... S.D. 78
185. ,, = Hierakonpolis . type 6 j S.D. 78
186. ,, = ,, . type 17 k ? S.D. 78
187. ,, = P.T. 1023 . . . S.D. 78

188. Alabaster . . . . type 8 c s.d. 81
189. ,, = Hierakonpolis.
190. ,, ,, . type 6 h s.d. 79
191. ,, = Hierakonpolis.
192. ,, = ,, . type 17 k s.d. 78
193. ,,
194. ,,
195. ,, = P.T. 1892 . . . . . s.d. 77
196. ,, = Hierakonpolis . type 14 n s.d. 79
197. ,,
198. ,, = P.T. 81 . . . . . s.d. 77
199. ,, ,, 1570 . . . . . s.d. 78
200. ,, = ,, 1627 . . . . . s.d. 77
201. ,, = Hierakonpolis . type 15 p s.d. 77
202. ,, = ,, . type 17 f s.d. 78
203. Red limestone . . . R.T. 70, 408 s.d. 79
204. Bk. basalt . . . R.T. xxxiii, 10 s.d. 80
205. Alabaster = P.T. 1023 . . . . . s.d. 78
206. ,, ... type 14 t s.d. 78
207. ,, = P.T. 1023 . . . . . s.d. 78
208. ,, ... type 14 t s.d. 78
209. Red porphyry . . . R.T. 88 s.d. 79
210. Basalt . . . . . R.T. 57 s.d. 79
211. Noble serpentine . . . R.T. 58 s.d. 79
212. Basalt [5] . . . . . R.T. 491 s.d. 79
213. ,, [7] . . . . . R.T. 59 s.d. 79
214. ,, [6] . . . . Ab. I, xliv, 2 s.d. 81
215. ,, [1] . . . . . R.T. 59 s.d. 79
216. ,, [2] . . . . . R.T. 70 s.d. 79
217. ,, ... Ab. I, xliii, 4 c s.d. 80
218. ,, [9] . . . . ,, 61 s.d. 80
219. Pink limestone [3]. s.d. 80

Plate XVII.

220. Slate . . . . . R.T. 292, 401 s.d. 80
221. Bk. wt. syenite . . . R.T. 51 s.d. 79
222. Bk. wt. porphyry . . R.T. 58 s.d. 79
223. Alabaster . . . . . R.T. 59 s.d. 79
224. Basalt . . . . . R.T. 59 s.d. 79
225. Gy. syenite . . . . Ab. I, xliii, 4 c s.d. 80
226. Slate = Abydos . . . R.T. 402 s.d. 79
227. Alabaster.
228. Slate . . . . . . R.T. 402 s.d. 80
229. ,, ... R.T. 245 s.d. 79
230. Pink limestone . . . R.T. 59 s.d. 79
231. Alabaster, triangular . R.T. xxxiii, 22 s.d. 80
232. Serpentine . . . G.R. v D, 61 . s.d. 80
233. Quartz crystal . . R.T. 195, 250 s.d. 79
234. Gy. steatite. . . G.R. v C, 34 . s.d. 80
235. Alabaster = P.T. 19 . . . . . s.d. 79
236. ,, = ,, 153 . . . . . s.d. 80
237. ,, = Gizeh G.R. v D, 73 s.d. 80
238. Gy. volcanic ash . . . R.T. 248 s.d. 80
239. Hard limestone . . Ab. I, xliii, 4 c s.d. 80
240. Bk. wt. syenite . . ,, ,, s.d. 80
241. Basalt . . . . . R.T. 69 s.d. 79
242. Alabaster . . . .type 14 n s.d. 79
243. Basalt . . . G.R. v D, 65 s.d 80
244. Dolomite . . . R.T. 165, 166 s.d. 79
245. Alabaster . . R.T. 426, 432 s.d. 80, 81
246. Slate . . . . G.R. v D, 77 s.d. 80
247. Gy. wt. metamorph. {G.R. v D, 62 s.d. 80; R.T. 109 . s.d. 81}

Plate XVIII.

248. Slate . . . . . . R.T. 207 s.d. 81
249. Alabaster . . . . . R.T. 293 s.d. 81
250. Pink limestone . . . type 6 q s.d. 82
251. Limestone = P.T. 231 . . . . . s.d. 81
252. ,, ... type 8 n . s.d. 81
253. Red limestone.
254. Gy. volcanic ash.
255. ,,
256. Drab, wt. alabaster . . type 8 r . s.d. 81
257. Alabaster.
258. Alabaster = P.T. 249 . . . . . s.d. 81
259. Pink limestone . . . type 8 r . s.d. 81
260. Quartz crystal.
261–2. Yell. gy. serpentine, oval.
263–4. Gy. volcanic ash, oval.
265. Gy. volcanic ash [74].
266. Alabaster, cf. P.T. I, xlvi, 11 b . s.d. 79–81
267. Red buff limestone . . R.T. 237 s.d. 81
268. Basalt [70] . . . . R.T. 52 s.d. 81
269. ,, [69] . . . . . ,, s.d. 81
270. Calcite = P.T. 61 . . . . . s.d. 81
271. Bk. wt. porphyry [67] . R.T. 62, 91. s.d. 81
272. Alabaster . . . R.T. 62, 95. s.d. 81
273. Slate . . . R.T. 242 ; type 13 p s.d. 81
274. Bk. wt. syenite . . . R.T. 91 s.d. 81
275. Gypsum.
276. Pink alabaster . . . type 13 f, g s.d. 81
277. Bk. wt. porphyry. . . R.T. 93 s.d. 81

Plate XIX.

278. Alabaster . . . . . R.T. 95 s.d. 81
279. Basalt . . R.T. 421, 63 s.d. 81, 82
280. Alabaster . R.T. 107 ; Ab. I, xlv, 7 s.d. 81
281. ,, ... Ab. I, xlvii, 31 s.d. 82
282. Buff limestone . . . type 14 m s.d. 81
283. Alabaster . . . . type 18 t s.d. 81
284. Pinkish limestone . . R.T. 432 s.d. 81
285. Slate . . . . Ab. I, xliv, 52 s.d. 81
286. Alabaster . Ab. I, xliv, 40 ; xlvii, 5 s.d. 81
287. Bl. gy. volcanic ash . . R.T. 220 s.d. 81
288. Hard limestone . . . R.T. 423 s.d. 81
289. Limestone . . . . . R.T. 427 s.d. 81
290. Bk. steatite . . . Ab. I, xliv, 40 s.d. 81
291. Bl. volcanic ash . . . R.T. 255 s.d. 81
292. Buff limestone, gy. veins Ab. I, xlvii, 21 s.d. 81

293. Alabaster = P.T. 250 — S.D. 81
294. Bk. wt. syenite — R.T. 442 — S.D. 81
295. Slate — R.T. 227 — S.D. 81
296. Volcanic ash — R.T. 436 — S.D. 81
297. Alabaster = P.T. 250 — S.D. 81
298. Slate — R.T. 220 — S.D. 81
299. Alabaster — type 24 v — S.D. 81
300. Gy. volcanic ash — ,, — S.D. 81
301. Alabaster — R.T. 446, 473 — S.D. 81, 82
302. Alabaster [75] = Tarkhan 165 — S.D. 81
303. Alabaster — R.T. 266 — S.D. 81

Plate XX.

304. Hard limestone — R.T. 400, 486 — S.D. 82
305. Serpentine, altered — R.T. 400 — S.D. 82
306. Limestone — R.T. 486, 492 — S.D. 82
307. Aragonite — R.T. 143 — S.D. 82
308. Bl. volcanic ash — R.T. 147 — S.D. 82
309. Basalt — R.T. 63 — S.D. 82
310. Slate — R.T. 486 — S.D. 82
311. Bk. wt. porphyry [68] — R.T. 92 — S.D. 82
312. Bk. wt. limestone [72] — R.T. 92 — S.D. 82
313. Basalt [71] — R.T. 92 — S.D. 82
314. Gy. volcanic ash — R.T. 150 — S.D. 82
315. Alabaster.
316. Gy. volcanic ash — R.T. 150, 152 — S.D. 82
317. Buff bk. limestone — R.T. 490 — S.D. 82
318. Bl. volcanic ash — R.T. 149, 150 — S.D. 82
319. Buff limestone — R.T. 429, 467 — S.D. 82
320. Slate — R.T. 155 — S.D. 82
321. Slate — R.T. 451 — S.D. 82
322. Serpentine — R.T. 465 — S.D. 82
323. Alabaster — R.T. 257 — S.D. 82
324. ,, — R.T. 255, 258 — S.D. 81, 82
325. Gy. volcanic ash — R.T. 177 — S.D. 82
326. ,, ,, — R.T. 184 — S.D. 82
327. Diorite — R.T. 186 — S.D. 82
328. Basalt — ,, — S.D. 82

Plate XXI.

329. Alabaster — G.R. vi C, 102 — II
330. ,, — ,, 103 — II
331. ,, — ,, 103 — II
332. ,, — ,, 103 — II
333. ,, — ,, 103 — II
334. ,, — R.T. 161 — II
335. Bk. wt. porphyry — R.T. 110, 158 — II
336. — R.T. 158 — II
337. — G.R. vi D, 129; R.T. 110 — II
338. — R.T. 158, 160 — II
339. Bl. volcanic ash [88] — R.T. 173 — II
340. Bk. wt. syenite — Ab. I, ix, 14, Khosekhemui
341. ,, ,, — ,, — ,,
342. Gy. gneiss — ,, — ,,
343. Alabaster [15] — Ab. I, ix, 14, 15, Khosekhemui
344. Gy. porphyry — Ab. I, ix, 15 — ,,
345. Hornblende schist — G.R. vi E, 142 — III
346. White granite [90] — **Ab. I, ix, 15** — II

Plate XXII.

347. Alabaster — M.K. xxi, 6 — early III
348. ,, — M.K. xxi, 8 — ,, III
349. Gypsum — G.T. ix, 18 — ,, III
350. Hard limestone — M.K. xiv, 18 — ,, III
351. Limestone — M.K. xxi, 6 — ,, III
352. Hard limestone — M.K. xiv, 17 — ,, III
353. Alabaster — M.K. xxi, 6 — ,, III
354. Diorite — G.T. ix, 19 — ,, III
355. Alabaster — M.M. xxiv, 2 — III
356. Hard limestone — M.K. xxi, 6 — early III
357. Bl. volcanic ash — M.K. xxi, 11 — ,, III
358. Bk. steatite — M.K. xxi, 11 — ,, III
359. Alabaster = Khallaf. M.K. xxviii, 7 — ,, III
360. ,, — M.K. xii, 15 — ,, III
361. Porphyry — M.K. xii, 6 — ,, III
362. Pink limestone — M.K. xii, 16 — ,, III
363. Alabaster — M.K. xii, 16 — ,, III
364. Volcanic ash — G.T. viii, 3 — ,, III
365. Gypsum } see 972, Roman (?).
366. Gypsum }
367. Drab limestone.
368. Alabaster.
369. Alabaster.
370. ,, — ? G.T. viii, 2 — III
371. ,,

Plate XXIII.

372. Slate — G.R. vi D, 127 — III
373. Gy. volcanic ash — ,, — III
374. Diorite — ,, 123 — III
375. Diorite — ,, 129 — III
376. Alabaster — ,, 130, 131 — III
377. ,, — ,, 132 — III
378. Wt. quartz — ,, 130 — III
379. Alabaster — ,, 132 — III
380. Diorite — G.R. vi E, 143 — III
381. Alabaster — ,, 145 — III
382. ,, = Meydum. M. xxix, 15 — late III
383. Diorite — See M.M. xxvi, 43 — ,, III
384. Diorite [111] — Q. Kab, iii — ,, III
385. Diorite [114] — ,, III
386. Basalt [112] — Q. Kab, iii — ,, III
387. Alabaster [113] — ,, III
388. Buff limestone.
389. Alabaster.
390. Obsidian [117] — D. xxi — **VI**
391. Basalt [117] — Cem. Ab. I, iv — **VI**
392. ,, — ,, — **VI**
393. Bl. marble — Ab. III, xliv — **XVIII**

394. Diorite . . Ab. III, xliv .

395. Schist = Koptos XII

396. Alabaster.

PLATE XXIV.

397. Bk. steatite [120]

398. Alabaster [118]

399. Gy. volcanic ash

400. Limestone

401. Alabaster

402. Hard limestone

(397–402) types 13 k, 25 c . . S.D. 81

403. Serpentine [119] . . . type 13 k S.D. 81

404. Pink limestone.

405. Buff limestone . . . . . late II

406. ,, ,,

407. Aragonite.

408. Hard buff limestone.

409. Bl. marble.

410. Gypsum.

411. Alabaster.

412. ,,

413. Gy. limestone . Ab. I, ix, 11 . . late II

414. Alabaster . . ,,

415. Buff limestone

416. Wt. marble

417. Buff marble

(415–417) . . type 42 f S.D. 80, 81

418. Diorite.

419. Alabaster . . . . type 42 f S.D. 80

420. ,,

421. Bk. wt. syenite.

422. Buff limestone.

423. Bk. wt. marble.

424. Alabaster.

425. Breccia.

426. Alabaster . . . . type 42 g S.D. 81

427. Bk. bl. glaze . . . ,, S.D. 81

428. Alabaster . . . . ,, S.D. 81

429. Veined marble . . . ,, S.D. 81

430. Gy. wt. marble.

431. Ivory.

432. Alabaster.

433. ,, ... type 42 g S.D. 81

434. ,, = P.T. 191 . . . . S.D. 81

435. Volcanic ash.

436. Alabaster.

437. Breccia . . . . . type 34 S.D. 81

438. Dendritic limestone, see R.T. 201 . . S.D. 82

439. Limestone solid = Qa, Abydos . . S.D. 82

440. Bk. wt. syenite.

441. Alabaster.

442. Hard limestone.

443. Alabaster.

444. Gypsum.

445. Alabaster . . . . R.T. 121 S.D. 82

446. ,, ... M.K. xxvii, 6 III

447. Alabaster . . M.K. xxvii, 6 . III

448. Bk. wt. marble . ,, . III

PLATE XXV.

449. Alabaster [8] . . . T.R. 667 S.D. 79

450. ,, [131] . . . type 77 k S.D. 80

451. ,, = P.T. 153 . . . . S.D. 80

452. Gypsum . . . . type 77 s S.D. 80

453. ,, ... ,, S.D. 80

454. Alabaster banded.

455. ,, Abusir. . . . type 77 k S.D. 80

456. ,, see pot . type 85 c S.D. 77, 80

457. Pink limestone . . G.R. v C, 56 S.D. 80

458. Alabaster [142], . see pot type 94 L S.D. 79, 80

459. ,, [140] . . . type 77 k S.D. 80

460. ,, ... type 80 c S.D. 80

461. ,, [141] { . . type 80 c, f S.D. 80, 81 / . see pot type 94 l, m S.D. 80 }

462. ,, ,, ,, type 92 m S.D. 80

463. ,, [133] . . type 78 e S.D. 80, 81

464. ,, [134] . . . type 80 h S.D. 81

465. ,, [135] . . . ,, S.D. 81

466. [136] . . . R.T. 282 S.D. 81

467. Alabaster . . . . R.T. 282 S.D. 81

468. ,, [143] . . . type 80 c S.D. 80

469. ,, [137] . . type 78 k S.D. 80, 81

470. ,, = P.T. 165 . . . . S.D. 81

471. Gypsum = P.T. 191 . . . . S.D. 81

472. Alabaster [132] . . type 78 k S.D. 80, 81

473. ,, . . . ,, S.D. 80, 81

474. Gypsum = P.T. 191 . . . . S.D. 81

475. Alabaster . . . . type 78 s S.D. 81

476. ,, = P.T. 250 . . . . S.D. 81

477. ,, [138] . M.K. xxvii, 10 . III

PLATE XXVI.

478. Alabaster [152] . . . type 80 j S.D. 81

479. ,,

480. ,, [153]

481. ,, [154] type 81 b S.D. 81

482. Gypsum

483. ,,

484. ,, ... type 81 b S.D. 81

485. ,, fine . . . type 81 k S.D. 81

486. ,, [155] = P.T. 165 . . . S.D. 81

487. . . . . . type 81 k S.D. 81

488. Gypsum = P.T. 191 . . . . S.D. 81

489. Limestone = P.T. 250 . . . . S.D. 81

490. Alabaster = N.N.

491. Limestone, solid = Qa, Abydos . . S.D. 82

492. Buff bk. marble [148]. Ab. I, xi, 10. . end II

493. Bk. wt. marble [149] ,, . . ,, II

494. Gypsum.

495. ,, . . G.R. vi E, 143 . III

496. Buff limestone [146].

497. Gypsum.
498. Alabaster [145].
499. Gypsum.
500. Alabaster [150] . Ab. I, ix, 5 . . end II
501. Buff limestone . G.R. vii E ; Zaraby 36 VI
502. Gypsum.
503. Buff limestone.
504. Bk. wt. marble [147], see G.T. vii . . III
505. Alabaster [151] . M.K. xxxv, 18 . IV–VI

PLATE XXVII.

506. Alabaster [169] . M.K. xxxv, 6 . VI
507. ,, [171] . D. xxi ; G.R. vii E, 34 VI
508. ,,
509. Quartz crystal.
510. Alabaster.
511. ,, [158] = Memphis 1909. D. xxi VI
512. ,,
513. ,, [159] . M.K. xxxv, 13 . VI
514. ,, [170].
515. ,, . . M.K. xxxvi, 23 . VI
516. ,, . . See D.P. xxviii, Y 6 VI
517. ,, [172] . D. xxi . . . VI
518. ,, [173] . Zaraby 118 ; G.R. vii E VI
519. ,, . . D. xxi . . . VI
520. ,, . . D. xxi . . . VI
521. ,, . . M.K. xxxv, 1 . VI
522. ,, . . D.P. xxviii, Y 8 . VI
523. ,, . . Zaraby 35 ; G.R. vii E VI
524. ,, [174] . ,, ,, VI
525. ,, [176].
526. ,, . . Zaraby 57 ; G.R. vii E VI
527. ,, [175].
528. ,, [160] . D.P. xxviii . . VII
529. ,, = Zaraby 88, G.R. vii E, . VI
530. ,, . . D.P. xxviii, D 14 . VI
531. ,, [162] . ,, ,, . VI
532. ,, [161] . D.P. xxviii, 83 . VI
533. ,, [163].
534. ,, [164] . D.P. xxviii, Y 182 . IX
535. ,, [165]
536. ,, . . ? D. xxi. . . VI
537. Slate.
538. Bl. paste XII
539. Limestone, Abydos, Qa.. . . . . S.D. 82
540. Alabaster.
541. Sandstone . } D.P. xxx, Y 448 . XII
542. Alabaster . } G.R. xi A, 70 . XII
543. Alabaster.
544. Grey limestone.
545. Gy. bl. marble XII
546. Alabaster . . . . ? XII
547. Gy. bl. marble . G.A. ix . . . XII
548. Bk. steatite, polished.
549. Bk. steatite.

PLATE XXVIII.

550. Alabaster, solid ; and duplicate.
551. Limestone [167] D.P. xxviii, W 100 . VII
552. Alabaster, solid [168].
553. Limestone, solid = Abydos, Qa. . . S.D. 82
554. Diorite [166].
555. Diorite.
556. Limestone, solid = Abydos, Qa. . . S.D. 82
557. Alabaster = Harageh 360 . . . XII
558. ,, [177] . G.A. xviii, E 210 . ? XIV
559. ,, = D.P. xxviii . . . VII
560. ,, solid ; and duplicate.
561. ,, ,, ,,
562. Slate.
563. Limestone . . Cairo 408 . . XII
564. Alabaster [178].
565. ,, [179].
566. ,, [180].
567. ,, . . D. xxi . . . VI
568. ,, = Memphis. D.P. xxviii, N 19 VI
569. Limestone [182].
570. Alabaster [181].
571. ,, . . D. xx, 495, 509 . XI
572. Br. marble . . D.P. xxviii, Y 8 . VI
573. Pink buff marble [191], Abydos.
574. Alabaster.
575. ,,
576. ,, [190] = Mazghuneh l, 3 . XII
577. ,, [192] . Zaraby 53 ; G.R. vii E VI
578. ,, = Zaraby 118, G.R. vii E . VI
579. ,, [194] = Zaraby 37 ; G.R. vii E VI
580. ,, [193] as Zaraby 37 ; G.R. vii E VI
581. ,, . . M.K. xxxvi, 10, 11 . VI
582. ,, . . M.K. xxxvi, 10 . VI
583. ,, [184] . B. 12 ; D.P. W 83 VII
584. ,, [187] = Qurneh A 21 . . XI
585. ,, ... XI
586. ,, . . G.R. xi A, 34. . XI
587. Buff limestone [186].
588. ,, ,, D. xx, 32, 441 . VI–VIII
589. Alabaster = Qurneh A XI
590. ,, [185] = Qurneh A 56, D. xx, 441 XI
591. ,,
592. ,,
593. Buff limestone = Quft.
594. Alabaster.
595. Limestone . . D. xx, 274, 441 . VI–VIII
596. ,, = Qurneh B 20 . . . XI
597. Alabaster [188] . D. xxii, Antefaqer . XI
598. ,, [195] . D. xx, 32 ; xxii, Antefaqer XI
599. ,, { =Tarkhan 1747 + scarab . XI–XII
600. ,, { G.R. xi A, 194 { D.P. xxviii, Y 250
601. ,, [189]
602. ,, [183]

603. Alabaster = Qurneh B 24 . . . XI
604. Pink marble = Qurneh B 10 . . XI

PLATE XXIX.

605. Alabaster . . D.P. xxix, 348 . XII
606. ,, . . ,, . XII
607. ,, Abydos. D.P. xxx, 448 ; R.K. XII
608. ,,
609. ,,
610. ,, = Rifeh 215, G.R. xi A . . XII
611. ,, . . D.P. xxix, W 85 . XII
612. ,, . . { D.P. xxix, Y 51 . XII
Ab. III, xix, 10 . XVIII }
613. Bl. marble.
614. Buff marble
615. Bl. marble
616. Bl. glaze
617. Bl. marble
618. Alabaster
619. Bl. marble
620. Alabaster
621. ,,
622. Gy. bl. marble
(614–622: On nos. 613–626 compare *Diospolis*, xxix, xxx)
623. Bl. marble.
624. Gy. marble = Harageh 130.
625. Bk. bl. glaze.
626. Alabaster.
627. ,, = D.P. xxix, 152, R.K. . . XII
628. ,,
629. ,, . . D.P. xxix, W 32, 72 XII
630. ,, ,, XII
631. Bl. marble.
632. Alabaster.
633. Bl. marble. . . Ab. III, xi, 26 . XII
634. Alabaster.
635. ,, . . Cem. Ab. III, xiii . XII
636. ,,
637. ,,
638. ,, = Rifeh 257.
639. ,, = Harageh 645 . . . XII
640. ,, solid.
641. ,, ,,
642. ,, ,,
643. Bk. limestone = Harageh . . . XII
644. Alabaster, solid.
645. ,, ,,
646. Br. wt. marble.
647. Alabaster = Harageh 275 . . . XII
648. Alabaster = Harageh 275 . . . XII
649. Gypsum = Rifeh 243 ; G.R. xi A, R.K. . XII
650. Alabaster = Harageh 112 . . . XII
651. ,, = D.P. xxx, 361 ; Il. xiii, 3 XII
652. ,, = D.P. xxx, 361, 448 . . XII
653. ,,
654. ,, with kohl.
655. Alabaster
656. Bl. paste = Rifeh 243 ; G.R. xi A . XII
657. Alabaster = Harageh 92, R.K. . . XII
658. ,, . . D.P. xxx, Y 461, R.K. XII
659. ,, . . Cairo 18720, R.K. . XII
660. Alabaster = Bernasht XII
661. Alabaster . . G.R. xi A, 235 . XII
663. Gypsum = Rifeh 243, G.R. xi A . . XII
664. Alabaster.
665. Bk. serpentine = Koptos.
666. Pottery.
667. Bk. serpentine.
668. ,, ,, = Kahun
669. Alabaster = Kahun } group . . XII
670. Blue marble = Kahun
671. Alabaster = Gurob or Lahun.
672. Bk. serpentine = Gurob.
673. Alabaster = Lahun.
674. Olive glaze.
675. Gy. serpentine.
676. Limestone.
677. Alabaster = Kahun.
678. ,, = Lahun.

PLATE XXX.

679. Alabaster.
680. ,,
681. ,, = Harageh.
682. Bl. marble.
683. ,,
684. ,,
685. ,,
686. Alabaster.
687. Bl. marble.
688. Alabaster.
689. Bl. marble.
690. Serpentine.
691. ,,
692. ,,
693. Basalt.
694. Alabaster = Koptos.
695. ,, = Thebes.
696. ,,
693. Serpentine.
698. Limestone.
699. Alabaster.
700. ,,
701. Bl. marble = Rifeh 253, G.R. xi A . XII
702. Alabaster = Ramesseum.
703. ,, = Rifeh 67 (G.R. xxiii, 13)
704. ,, = Diospolis, W 114 ; G.R. xi A
705. Limestone = Qurneh, viii, 5 . . . XI
706. Serpentine = Abydos, Heqreshu.
707. Bl. marble = Diospolis, W 45.

708. Alabaster = Kahun, 1914 . . . XII
709. ,, = Harageh 275 . . . XII
710. Serpentine = Harageh 602 . . . XII
711. ,,
712. Steatite.
713. Alabaster = Diospolis 431.
714. ,, = Qurneh.
715. Serpentine.
716. Alabaster, inserted mouth.
717. Bl. marble.
718. ,,
719. Alabaster.
720. ,,
721. Limestone.
722. Serpentine.
723. Bl. marble.
724. Alabaster = Rifeh 116 ; G.R. xi A.
725. ,,
726. Bl. marble.
727. ,,
728. Alabaster . . down to here . ? XII
729. Serpentine = Qurneh from here on .? XVIII
730. Limestone.
731. Alabaster.
732. Limestone.
733. Alabaster.
734. Serpentine.
735. Alabaster.
736. Serpentine.
737. Alabaster.

PLATE XXXI.

738. Alabaster.
739. ,, = Rifeh 320 ; G.R. xxvii A.
740. ,, = Rifeh 231 ; ,,
741. Serpentine.
742. Alabaster = Rifeh.
743. ,,
744. ,,
745. Limestone.
746. ,,
747. Bl. marble.
748. Limestone, of Aufhensi . . . . ? XXI
749. Serpentine.
750. Alabaster.
751. Wood.
752. ,,
753. ,,
754. ,,
755. Limestone XVIII
756. Bone XVIII
757. ,, . . . A.A. xlvii, D 115 . XVIII
758. ,, . . . ,, ,, . XVIII
759. ,, . . . ,, ,, . XVIII
760. Wood XVIII
761. Bone XVIII
762. Wood.
763. ,,
764. ,,
765. Ivory.
766. Wood.
767. Bk. steatite.
768. Steatite = Koptos.
769. Bk. steatite . . . . . Roman

PLATE XXXII.

770. Gy. serpentine . Tehutmes III . XVIII
771. Alabaster.
772. ,,
773. Slate.
774. Alabaster.
775. ,,
776. ,,
777. ,,
778. Wt. marble.
779. Alabaster.
780. ,,
781. ,,
782. ,, . . . R.M. xiv, 62 . . XVIII
783. ,,
784. ,,
785. ,, = Pasar, G.R. xxiii, 46 . . XIX
786. ,,
787. ,,
788. ,,
789. ,, . . . Il. xviii, 25 . . XIX
790. ,, = Gurob.
791. ,, . . . Il. xvii, 31 . end XVIII
792. ,,
793. ,, = Nubt. N. 69, sect. 112. . XIX
794. Bk. steatite.
795. Alabaster.
796. ,,
797. ,,
798–806. Limestone painted, one group . XVIII
807. Alabaster.
808. Bk. steatite.
809. Wt. br. steatite.
810. Wt. steatite.
811. Alabaster.
812. Bk. steatite.
813. Alabaster [207].
814. ,, [202] . Cem. Ab. III, x, 6 . XVIII
815. ,, [208].
816. ,, [203] . A.A. li, D 77 . . XVIII
817. ,, [209] . A.A. xlix, D 9 Tehutmes III
818. ,, = Amarna XVIII
819. ,, [201].

PLATE XXXIII.

820. Alabaster = Koptos.
821. ,, [212].
822. ,, [205].
823. ,, [197] . L.G. xvi . . XVIII
824. ,,
825. { Buff limestone [196], Il. xxvii, 13 / Amenhetep II, P.G. II, xxiii, 33 } XVIII
826. Alabaster . . Cem. Ab. III, x, 6 . XVIII
827. Bk. bl. serpentine [206].
828. Alabaster.
829. ,, = Amarna . . . XVIII
830. ,, [198].
831. ,, [199] = Koptos.
832. ,, [210] Il. xvii, 10 . . XVIII
833. ,, K. xviii, 6 . . . XVIII
834. ,, [211] Amenhetep II, P.G. II, xxiii, 30.
835. ,, [204].
836. ,, Il. xviii, 23 . . XIX
837. ,, [200].
838. Limestone.
839. Breccia.
840. Alabaster.
841. ,,
842. ,, = Gurob. Cairo 18450, 18790 . XVIII
843. ,, Il. xxvii, 42 . . . XVIII
844. ,, = Rifeh 257, G.R. xxvii A . XIX
845. Limestone . R. xiv, 61 . . . XVIII
846. Alabaster . Il. xxvii, 5 . . XVIII
847. Br. serpentine ,, 3 . . XVIII
848. Alabaster.
849. Gy. br. serpentine. Il. xxvii, 2 . . XVIII
850. Alabaster . Cem. Ab. III, xii, 11 . XVIII
851. ,,
852. ,,
853. ,, . Il. xxvii, 6 . . . XVIII
854. ,,
855. ,, . A.A. 1; D. 17, Tehutmes III.
856. ,,
857. ,,
858. ,,
859. ,,

PLATE XXXIV.

860. Alabaster.
861. ,,
862. ,,
863. ,, { = L. xvi, 2, 61 . . . . XVIII / Amenhetep II; P.G. II, xxii, 14 }
864. ,,
865. ,, . Il. xx, 11 . . late XVIII
866. Bk. serpentine. Il. xviii, 51; xix, 11 XIX
867. Alabaster . Amenhetep III . . XVIII
868. Bk. steatite . Il. xxvi, 48 . . . XVIII
869. Alabaster . Yuaa xxv . . . XVIII
870. Alabaster
871. ,,
872. ,, { Tehutmes III; Il. xxvii, 7 / Amenhetep II; P.G. II, xxii, 21 }
873. ,,
874. ,,
875. ,,
876. ,, { as pot, Cem. Ab. II, xxi, 7; p. 105 . . . . XVIII / or R.M. xiv, 63 . . . ? XXII }
877. ,, = Rifeh 175; G.R. xxvii A . XVIII
878. ,, L.G. xvi; Amenhetep III.
879. ,,
880. Serpentine = Meydum. L.G. xvi, 3 . XVIII
881. Alabaster
882. ,,
883. ,, Cairo 18378, 18734 . . XVIII
884. ,,
885. ,, = Tutankhamen, K. xviii 25 XVIII

PLATE XXXV.

886. Alabaster Il. xvii, 41 XVIII
887. ,, = Gurob.
888. ,,
889. ,,
890. ,,
891. ,,
892. ,,
893. ,,
894. ,,
895. ,, later than L.G. xvi, 3 . . XVIII
896. Limestone.
897. Alabaster.
898. ,, Il. xix, 19 XIX
899. ,, = Meydum; L.G. xvii, 16.
900. ,,
901. ,,
902. ,,
903. ,,
904. ,,
905. ,,
906. ,,
907. ,, G.A. xxi, 155; Hatshepsut.
908. ,, with gold mounting.
909. ,, Ramessu II.
910. ,,
911. ,,
912. ,,
913. ,,
914. ,, = Gurob; Il. xix, 36.

PLATE XXXVI.

915. Alabaster Il. xvii, 42 XVIII
916. ,,

917. Alabaster { with gold mount and silver foot. Ramessu II and Nefertari . XIX
918. Alabaster = Gurob ; K. xviii, 1 . . XIX
919. ,, Sety II ; Il. xix, 25 . . XIX
920. ,, = Thebes
921. ,, = Memphis ; Ptah temple
922. ,,
923. ,,
924. ,,
925. ,,
926. ,,
927. ,,
928. ,,
929. Slate.
930. Serpentine.
931. Limestone . . . . ? VI
932. Bk. steatite.
933. Serpentine. H. xix, 85 . . . ? XXIII
934. Alabaster.
935. ,, ? see D.P. xxix, Y 51 . ? XII
936. ,,
937. ,,
938. ,,
939. ,,
940. Basalt.

Plate XXXVII.
941. Alabaster, yellow,
942. ,, ,, = Abusir.
943. ,,
944. ,,
945. ,,
946. ,,
947. Pottery, source of type, H. xvii A . . XXII
948. Alabaster.
949. ,,
950. ,,
951. ,, Cairo 18490, Psamtek I . XXVI
952. ,,
953. ,,
954. ,,
955. ,,
956. ,, = Fayum, Edwards.
957. ,,
958. ,, } Palace of Apries, xvi, 1, 2 . XXVI
959. ,,
960. ,,
961. ,,
962. Gypsum.
963. Alabaster.
964. ,,
965. ,, Edwards Coll.
966. ,, very thin, F.T. x, late Ptolemaic.
967. ,, ,, ,, ,,
968. ,, B. Mus., Wilk. 275, Nekau . XXVI

969. Alabaster = Kafr Ammar . . 1st cent. A.D.
970. ,,
971. ,, = Mazghuneh, xlvi . 1st cent. A.D.

Plate XXXVIII.
972. Alabaster = Mazghuneh xlvi . . . 1st cent.
973. ,, ,, ... ,,
974. Bk. steatite.
975. Steaschist.
976. Gypsum.
977. Slate.
978. Br. serpentine = Koptos.
979. Bk. granite.
980. Alabaster, pestle, Cairo 18255.
981. ,,
982. Basalt, Cairo 18736, Psamtek II.
983. Alabaster, Cairo 18248.
984. Gy. steatite.
985. Gy. serpentine.
986. Gy. syenite (see 365–6).
987. Gy. serpentine.
988. Br. steatite.
989. Gy. steatite.
990. Br. serpentine.
991. Serpentine.
992. Alabaster, Mazghuneh, xlvi . . . 1st cent.
993. ,, ,, ,,
994. ,,
995. ,,
996. Gy. steatite.
997. Basalt.

Of these 997 drawings, 24 are not of stone ; there are thus 973 stone vases drawn, besides duplicates of some forms.

METAL VASES

INTRODUCTION

36. *Materials.* Regarding the metal vases, much of what has been already stated about the catalogue of stone vases is similarly applicable, and the first three sections of the introduction apply to both.

As to the materials, the metal vases in the earlier dynasties are all of copper. This is usually hammered, figs. 8, 9, but as early as Khosekhemui, of the iind dynasty, the spouts of the vases were cast by *cire perdue* (fig. 4), and then attached to hammered vases, or set in a fresh wax vase-body and so joined in a second *cire perdue* casting (fig. 3).

A curious mixture of work is seen in the xviiith dynasty, the cup 18 having the bronze bowl hammered very thin and elastic, and then fitted with a wax stem and foot, rising through a hole in the base of the bowl for the *cire perdue* casting here. The bronze bowl 20 shows another interesting piece of work. In the hammering out of it, the sharp edge of the foot broke through, around half the circuit; this has been mended by flushing it with melted bronze of the same quality, and grinding off the surplus outside. The funnel and flask, 25, 26, show a curious mixture, the bodies being of yellow bronze, while the top ribbed part of the funnel and the brim of the flask are of red copper.

Silver is rarely found, the only large groups being those from Mendes and Bubastis. Here there are two bowls, 30, 31. The former was made by spinning the metal, as shown by the lines on it, its thinness and its hardness. The latter was probably cast, as it is rather thick and soft. The octagonal vase of Roman age, 138, is of silver, with gold neck and handles. One gold vase here, 24, is entirely hammered or burnished work, with impressed relief and lines.

The pewter work is of Roman age; the dippers 124, 125 have pewter bowls and iron stems; they were found with the pewter bowls 142, 143, and three others similar, and a bronze bowl, 141. Plain lead was used in one case for the dipper 121. Iron once appears, for the brazier 135, pierced with triangular air holes.

37. *Manufacture.* The methods of manufacture have been partly noted above. A very difficult piece of work is seen in no. 15, which has no trace of a joint nor of spinning lines. It is so thin that *cire perdue* casting is improbable; yet the long neck being only a quarter of the diameter of the body, the introduction of a hook tool, to beat it on, seems unlikely. It would be just possible to pass in a hook tool ¼ of an inch deep, to support any part of the upper half of the body. The *hes* vase, 68, of the xxist dynasty has been clumsily made in two parts, which have been joined askew. In the Roman age *cire perdue* was kept up, as seen in the measure 102. This is of a single casting, body, handle, and three feet, with a thick brim, and three raised bands on the inside to divide the contents in four equal parts.

The Graeco-Roman fashion of making very thin bronze vessels, with heavy solid-cast handles attached later, was not happy in the effect, and is most disastrous for their preservation. The thin bronze rots and the weight of the heavy handles breaks it up as soon as it is moved. The complete form is seen in 100; in 99 the handle has become detached, leaving traces of its fixing; often loose handles are found, as 132, 133, 134, without any vessel.

The use of solder is rare in Egyptian work. A ring in the bottom of bowl 34 is soldered in, and seems to be original work of the xviiith dynasty. Riveting was the usual way of fixing handles, as on 16, 17, 25, 39, 40, 45, 50. But solder must have been used for the calf figure 44, as it has no rivet holes; and this seems to be of the xviiith–xxth dynasties. Soldering became usual in the Greek age for the massive handles then used; but it was so poorly done, owing to not cleaning the joint, that the true alloying was only very partial and readily broke away. Pliny, indeed, confuses the adhesion of marble by resin with the cleansing of lead by resin in order that solder should alloy with it.

CHAPTER VII

DYNASTIC VASES

38. Pl. XXXIX. *Vases of the ist–xiith dynasties.* As the metal vases are much fewer than those of stone, and there are fewer details of material and references to be noted, the current description here renders a listed catalogue unnecessary. The question of the contents is dealt with in the catalogue of *Ancient Weights and Measures.*

1. Spout made of sheet copper, bent to the form, and with fixing flanges made by turning the sides outwards (Khosekhemui tomb, iind dynasty).

2. Spout made by *cire perdue* casting, with a continuous flange, ready for fixing it in a vase (Khosekhemui).

3. Vase with long curved spout, with flange sloping to an edge. The flange section is drawn in open outline, the vase body section in solid black. A similar length of spout is shown in Rahetep's offerings (*Medum*, xiii).

4. Double spout; made by modelling two spouts separately in wax, joining them into one flange, and casting the whole by *cire perdue* (Khosekhemui, dyn. ii).

5. Vase with broken spout; square-edged flange. Apparently both 3 and 5 had the spout cast first and then inserted in a wax moulding for casting the whole vase. Spouted metal vases of this kind were

used for washing as early as the beginning of the ist dynasty (palette of Narmer), and are stated to be for washing, at the tomb of Methen (*L.D.*, ii, 4).

6. Model vase, cast *cire perdue*, for a tomb offering.

7. Vase cast *cire perdue*. The form of spout is the same as on a piece of blue glazed vase from the royal tombs at Abydos, so this is probably of the early dynasties.

8. Bowl of beaten copper from Tarkhan, 16, S.D. 78. The edge is roughly turned down outwards, to stiffen it.

9. Platter of beaten copper, with a hollow in the middle. Very roughly made as one of a large quantity of funeral models. Khosekhemui tomb.

10, 11. Bowls of cast copper, usual from the iind to the vith dynasties; see *R.T.*, ix, 13, 15, and Cairo Catalogue, 3480. They were also imitated in pottery, probably in the vth–vith dynasties (*Cem. Abyd.* I, ii). 10, 11 are the usual hammered basins of the iind–vith dynasties.

12. Conical cup of roughly hammered copper, having about 40 strokes in the height of it.

13. Cup of similar work, with hole in the base. This has evidently had the previous cup put over the mouth of it, as the marks and corrosion exactly agree. As there is no sign of intentional junction or union, the collocation was probably merely made to keep them clean inside. The hole in the base was probably for casting on a foot, as on 18, and the work of both of these was left unfinished.

39. *Vases of the xviiith dynasty.* 14. Bowl of beaten bronze, with incised pattern. The handle is of hammered wire, tapered to the end, and with the thin ends wound round the shanks. It is passed through a cast holder, which is riveted on to the bowl.

15. Flask of bronze, inscribed for the "washer of the sandals of Amen, Tehuti-hetep." The form was degraded in the xixth dynasty (*Dendereh* xxiv, 2), and it is reflected in pottery about Tehutmes IV (*Gizeh and Rifeh*, xxvii, K, 383), and degraded under Sety II (*Illahun* xix, 13). The surface has been finished by scraping, to remove traces of hammering. The thickness is only $\frac{1}{40}$ inch on an average, as shown by the weight not exceeding 7 ounces.

16. Jug of bronze, beaten in one piece, with cast handle riveted on. The handle ends above in a lotus pattern.

17. Cast bronze lotus handle, from a jug with a shorter neck. Such handles are of the xviiith–xixth dynasties (see *Amrah and Abydos*, xlvi, D 116; xliv, D 33).

18. Bronze cup, hammered, very thin and still quite elastic. A hole has been made in the bottom of the bowl, and a foot cast on it by *cire perdue*. The foot is hollow below, as marked by section line.

19. Bronze bowl from Gurob. The foot and swell in the side, and the slight lip, belong to pottery of the time of Hatshepsut (see *Gizeh and Rifeh*, xxvii H, 222, 228).

20. Bronze bowl of the xixth dynasty, from Dendereh (*D.*, xxiv, 8). In hammering it the bottom edge broke through, and it has been united by a flush of melted bronze.

21. Bowl of bronze hammered, with slightly raised centre. The form is an advance on the Hatshepsut form 19. Rough red patina.

22. Dish of bronze, with umbo centre, around which is an incised pattern, shown here above. The umbo, for a finger under the bowl when in use, began to be made as early as Tehutmes III, as in the gold bowl of Tehuti in Paris. This bowl is rather later than that.

23. A strange combination of a bronze cylindrical body with a shoulder and neck of blue glaze fitted into it. On the body is incised "fraction $\frac{1}{8}$," and this contains $\frac{1}{8}$ of the *hen* of $28\frac{1}{2}$ or 29 cubic inches, as measured to the top of the neck or to the brim.

24. Gold vase with relief-work bust on each side, probably intended for Hathor. The neck has been made in one piece, and the body as a separate piece; the neck and body were soldered together, and the rings at the sides were also soldered on. The face and arms are in relief, the crossing lines of the hair are incised. I bought it from a local dealer at Hawara, in a crushed condition; but as the gold is very soft, it was easily put back into its original form (xviiith or xixth dynasty).

25. Bronze funnel; with upper sixth of thin copper, having two raised bands to stiffen it. There was formerly a small handle, the bottom of which remains riveted on, and two rivet holes show in the copper band above. The form evidently was influenced by the Cretan conical vases.

26. Bronze flask, with narrow band of copper round the lip. Earlier stages of the same form are seen in pottery under Tehutmes IV (*G.R.*, xxvii K, 380, 386). This and no. 25 were found together, and probably belong to the time of Akhenaten. I bought them in Cairo, much crushed and burnt black; there was, however, a metallic body below the

black oxide of copper. By heating red hot and quenching in alcohol several times, Miss Burke (of University College) restored the whole to a metallic state, and I was then able to bend both vessels back to their original form.

27. Bronze drinking vessel, dated to Hatshepsut by the parallel form in pottery (*G. and R.*, xxvii H, 253).

28. Bronze drinking vessel. This form is of the same age (see *G. and R.*, xxvii H, 241) ; the earlier varieties of the form are more pointed (*G. and R.*, xxvii D, 49–59).

29. A larger bronze drinking vessel of about the time of Amenhetep II (see *G. and R.*, xxvii K, 346).

40. Pl. XL. *Vases of the xixth–xxth dynasties.* 30. Silver bowl, with incurved brim and slightly raised centre. It was formed by spinning, as shown by the lines on the face. The purpose of this form was doubtless for a finger-bowl, carried round byservants at meals, the edge being inturned to prevent spilling the water. This was found with the next dish in one of the great silver groups at Bubastis, and is thus dated to the xixth dynasty.

31. Silver dish, with umbo centre. This is rather thick and soft, and therefore seems to have been cast (Bubastis, xixth dynasty).

32. Bronze dish, with umbo. This is thin and flexible, and a good deal twisted.

33. Bronze dish, with wide umbo.

34. Bronze dish, with thickened edge, and a short tube soldered in the centre, probably to hold a central ornament.

35, 36, 37. Bronze bowls, hammered very thin. From the good work, these may be of the xviiith dynasty.

38. Bronze dish, rather thick.

39. Bronze dish, the centre punched through and soldered. On the side an attachment for a handle, riveted on.

40. Bronze dish, very thin, with riveted attachment for a handle.

41, 42. Bronze bowls.

43. One of three similar bronze bowls, stuck together by corrosion.

44. Loop handle for a bowl, with attachment in the form of a couchant calf. Bronze.

45. Attachment for a handle, in the form of a hand, with rivets. Bronze.

46–48. Bronze strainers, for pouring wine through.

49. Bronze dish with slight foot, descended from the form 19.

50. Bronze dish with loop handle, riveted attachment. This is descended from the form 20 of the xixth dynasty, and hence from 19 of the xviiith. It is from the tumuli of the xxth dynasty at Tell el Yehudiyeh, 1887.

51, 52. Bronze bowls, also dated to the xxth dynasty, from the tumuli of Yehudiyeh. These seem to be the first of the deep form with thickened edge.

53. Bronze bowl of the previous form, and therefore of the xxth dynasty.

54. Bronze bowl with thick edge but no projection. This is the Assyrian type of 700 B.C. (Botta, *Ninive*, 37, 98, No. 4, 126).

41. *Necked bowls.* This class of bronze bowl is evidently later than the xxth dynasty forms which we have just noted. They seem to start from 59 like an alabaster bowl of Tehutmes III (*G.R.*, xxvii A, 26). A flat form, most like 62, occurs in a North Syrian cemetery with objects beginning at about 700 B.C. (*Anc. Egypt*, 1917, 41). Yet there is no evidence of this form belonging to the rich and flourishing xxvith dynasty, unless the silver bowls of Mendes are placed to that age. Altogether we cannot yet limit it more closely than 1000 to 500 B.C., though probably about 700–600 B.C.

55. This bronze flask is similar to xviiith dynasty forms (*G. and R.*, xxvii L, 421). It is placed here as a type which influenced, or originated, the necked bowls. A variant of it, half-way between these, is from the xviiith dynasty tomb D 29 at Abydos (*Amrah and Abydos*, xlviii, mid top right hand). Another, and perhaps more direct, influence on these bowls was the form 50, of the xxth dynasty.

56 is a small bowl, partly crushed at the top.

57 to 67. As 67 is, by the lines, obviously the latest in style—late Greek, or possibly Roman—the sharp shoulder is a late feature. This agrees with the gentle rounding of the prototypes 20, 50. Hence these bowls are placed with the roundest shoulders first and the increasing angularity later. As 60 and 66 are on the Persian standard of volume, the form may be Eastern.

42. Pl. XLI. *Vases of the xxist–xxvith dynasties.* 68. Bronze *hes* vase from the burial of Nesitaneb-asheru at Deir el Bahri, about 970 B.C. The upper part and base, made separately, have been joined together carelessly askew. The inscription is " The Osiris, the great chief, the head of the harym of Amen Ra, king of the gods, Nesi-ta-neb-asheru."

69. The series of pendant situlae, 69–74, is the

commonest type of later times. The earliest fixed example appears to be that in the main group at Dendereh (*Dend.*, xxiv, 10), which is probably of the xixth dynasty; it is copied here in the small figure marked 1 : 6. This is obviously descended from the large drinking jar of the xviiith dynasty, such as those under Amenhetep II (*G. and R.*, xxvii K, 352, 356), but provided with metal loops for a handle, instead of cord loops which were probably used on the pottery jars for suspension. By about the xxiind dynasty the top had contracted much, as in 69, which is of hammered work, with a stout casting for the mouth and loops. A rougher form was made with the handle merely passing through holes in the neck, as in 70. The mass of small situlae as 71–74 are of the xxiind to xxvith dynasties, as shown by the names of dedicators upon them; those in the Cairo Museum have names of Nesi-ba-neb-zedu (xxi), Nesimin and Nesikhonsu (xxii), Zed-ptah-auf-onkh (xxii), Mertheru (xxiii), Psemthek and Haa-abra (xxvi). The form 73 is certainly late, as such was found with much worn alabastra at Dendereh.

The series of bronze cylinders, 75–80, appear to be measures, and similar cylinders were made of pottery. The whole question of measures is dealt with in the Catalogue of *Weights and Measures*, in which such vases as agree with known standards are repeated in the plates. 75 is of thin beaten bronze. 76 is likewise beaten, with a sloping spout projecting; but it is kept up to full level at the top edge to hold the liquid. The three regular cylinders, 77–79, are in the proportion of 5 : 3 : 2, the basis being the Syrian *kotyle*. The same form in pottery belongs to about 600 B.C. at Defenneh (*Tanis* II, xxxv, 75, 76).

The series of little bronze cylinders with handles, 83–89, was found together at Nubt, of uncertain age. The purpose of them was for measuring gold dust, and when piled full they contain $\frac{1}{2}$, $\frac{1}{4}$, $\frac{1}{8}$, $\frac{1}{16}$, $\frac{1}{32}$, $\frac{1}{64}$, $\frac{1}{128}$ of the *deben*. The last is the Ethiopian *pek* of gold, mentioned on the stele of Hersiatef. This system of gold measuring is therefore known to have been used in Ethiopia. The average *deben* given by these is 1,486 grains, and the mean error of the measures is $6\frac{1}{2}$ grains (see *Naqada*, p. 67). These measures were cast, and then ground down at the top to contain the exact quantity.

81 and 82 are two small bronze measures, perhaps also for gold dust. 81 contains the same as 89 within $\frac{1}{16}$.

90. Bronze jug, cast *cire perdue*. The modelling is very regular, and with flat even surfaces of brim and spout. Probably early Greek period.

91, 92. Bronze dishes, of which there are no dated examples. On reference to the pottery, the nearest parallel is of 600 B.C. from Defenneh (*Tanis* II, xxxv, 54), but with small handles. Other forms, rather more curved, were in the store rooms of Sety I, with pottery of about 600 B.C. (*Qurneh*, liv, 814, 819). The thickened edge with flat brim is like that of the Yehudiyeh bowls, 52, 53, of 1100 B.C., and is not found in Greek vessels. On this ground it is likely that these bronze dishes may be of about 800 B.C., and the later pottery forms imitate them.

93, 94. Bronze pans with handles. These are found in groups with mirrors, and belong to the toilet; yet they are certainly not mirrors, as they are much thicker and far too concave. They seem to have been for heating some oil or unguents, with a thick body of metal to retain the heat while in use. They began to be used in the xviiith dynasty (*Abyd.* III, xvii), and were then wider at the junction of the handle. They were similar in the xxiiird dynasty (*Cem. Abyd.* III, xi, 1; see pot, vi, 38); but narrower in the handle in the xxvith dynasty (see *Tanis* II, xxxix, 6, 7). Fig. 93 is probably of the latter date; fig. 94, by the triangular papyrus-stem handle, the lotus-flower outline, and the more varied contour, seems earlier, perhaps xixth dynasty.

CHAPTER VIII

VASES OF GRAECO-ROMAN AGE

43. Pl. XLII. *Hydreia and measures.* Fig. 95. Bronze dish, thin and well made; a handle has been lost, shown by three rivet holes. The form is not dated in metal; but it seems to be Ptolemaic by the analogous pottery forms (*Hyksos Cities*, xxxix H, 224, 228, 253, 272, 331). Later stages of the type occur in Italy (see Tarbell, *Catalogue of Bronzes in Field Museum*, fig. 13, and later at Pompeii, fig. 115 A).

96. Bronze jug measure.

97, 98. Bronze vases, probably measures. The forms are those of the 1st cent. A.D., but Roman examples always have handles (Tarbell, *Cat.*, 130, 145).

99. Bronze vase, handle lost, leaving traces, here marked on neck and shoulder. This was made entirely by spinning, and is beautifully thin and light;

by the weight the average thickness is $\frac{1}{30}$ inch. It is probably of the ivth century B.C.

100. Bronze jug, of thin beaten metal, with heavy solid cast handle. The spout is lost, only the socket remaining. This was bought with the large basin 101, and these doubtless belonged together for washing purposes. The very wide neck suggests that it was also intended for pouring a big flush of water, as well as for a small stream by the spout. From the clumsy form, it is unlikely to be earlier than the iind century A.D. and might well be of the iiird century, but it does not seem as late as the Constantine style.

101. Bronze basin, accompanying the jug 100.

102. Bronze measure of two *hen*, divided by lines round the inside into 4 half *hen*. The whole has been modelled in wax and cast *cire perdue* in one piece. Roman.

103. Bronze jug measure of Egyptian style, but late.

104. Bronze jug measure. Roman.

105, 106. Bronze jug measures of Roman style, about the 1st century A.D. (see Tarbell, *Antiquities from Boscoreale*, cxl, 24406.

Pl. XLIII. 107. Bronze strainer, with handle ending in a duck's head. Early Roman.

108. Bronze vase of fish form, with two loops, above and below the mouth, for suspending it. Roman.

109. Spouted vase of bronze; a thick casting *cire perdue*. Part of the bottom edge is broken away. Roman.

110. Bronze dish, of beaten work. Handle with lion's head in a foliated base, cast solid and riveted into the side of the dish; another handle has been lost from the opposite side. Roman.

111. Bronze basin of Egyptian style. It appears to descend from the type of pottery basins of the xviiith dynasty (*G. and R.*, xxvii D, 1, 227, 399), which very probably lasted on to Ptolemaic times (*Hyk. Cities*, xxxix J, 333). Though there is no clear dating for this, it might perhaps be best put in the Persian period, before Greek influence was dominant.

44. *Group from Abydos.* Figs. 112 to 117 are one group of bronzes found together at Abydos; they are all much broken up by corrosion, and the form is not certain where the outlines are dotted. The value of them is in showing a set of contemporary forms. The decoration on 113 is of Ptolemaic age; but the lotus flower at the spring of the handle is more of the style of the vth century B.C., which hinders dating this in the late Ptolemaic or Roman age. The other vessels point to an earlier rather than a later date. 114 is like the xixth dynasty vase (*Dendereh*, xxiv, 1); 115 is like the Assyrian bowls of 700 B.C.; 116 has had a foot or stand, by traces below it, and it is like a great Assyrian *lebes* on a stand, 700 B.C. (Botta, *Ninive*, 76), except that it has handles. A similar brim and handle survived at Pompeii (Tarbell, *Cat.*, 234). Altogether about 300 B.C. would be a middle date for the group. This takes back the duck's-head pattern, on 113, 117, earlier than might be supposed otherwise.

112. Bronze cooking pot, with iron handle.

113. Bronze strainer with wreath, scroll, and lotus patterns.

114. Bronze cooking pot.

115. Bronze bowl, three alike.

116. Bronze *lebes* with two opposite handles cast solid: the handles are here put at right angles to show the two views. On the base are traces of a circular foot or stand, the limits of which are here marked by lines. Compare the Assyrian form (Botta, 76).

45. Pl. XLIV. *Dippers.* Fig. 117. Dipper, cast bronze, solid, with duck's head.

This concludes the group from Abydos.

118, 119. Bronze dippers, with ducks' heads and bands on the stems.

120. Bronze dipper with horse's head on the handle and foliated stem. This marks the beginning of the hook turning to the same side as the bowl, probably of the 1st century A.D.

121. Lead dipper; the stem is a strip twisted in the middle. Rifeh.

122. Bronze dipper with catches on the backs of the stem.

123. Bronze dipper, with stem in two parts, sliding one on the other. This was in order to adapt it to different depths of a jar.

124, 125. Pewter dippers with iron stems. These are examples of the very unusual soldering on iron. With these were bought 141–143.

126. Cast bronze cup, on three feet, with ribbed surface, perhaps a measure.

127, 128. Cast bronze cups, on three feet. Roman.

46. *Handles.* Fig. 129. Large bronze handle of a situla ending in birds' heads. Cast.

130. Handle from a *lebes*, with fore-parts of horses. Cast bronze.

131. Small bronze handle of a jug.

132. Bronze handle with two hands to attach to a *lebes*. Cast imperfect.

133. Attachment for lifting a bowl, without any ring. Bronze, Egyptian.

134. Bronze handle, cast solid.

135. Small iron brazier, pierced with triangular holes. Broken.

136. Bronze basis, for a vase or a statue. The upper part circular, spreading out to a square foot.

47. *Late vases.* Fig. 137. Small cup of cast bronze, with ribbed outside.

138. Octagonal silver vase, with neck and handles thickly plated with gold. The polygonal form was favoured in the ivth–vith centuries A.D.; the simplicity and good style of this would place it early in that class. From Thebes.

139. Bronze cup with arching pattern around the base. Cast.

140. Bronze vessel, probably for heating wine. Half the top is covered, and the rest had a hinging lid, now lost. A spout has also been lost, only the hole for it showing here. The lid and end of the handle missing and the top bent inward.

141. Bronze bowl with slightly raised centre; bought with the two dippers 124, 125, and five pewter bowls, as 142, 143.

142, 143. Pewter bowls, and three others between the sizes of these, one with the bottom rusted away. The condition of most of this group of pewter is fresh and bright. Roman.

144. Bronze bowl of late Arab work, with incised inscriptions. Placed here to show the survival of the umbo, which began in the xviiith dynasty.

145. Censer of bronze open work. The body in a single casting, with twisted handle, now partly broken away. The lid a single casting, hinged to the body. Not figured.

146. Bronze censer, with perforated dome lid and perforated edge to the cup below. The form is evidently copied from an Arabic dome; in outline and in pattern it most resembles that of the tomb of Bars Bey, A.D. 1438. These perforated censers may then be dated to about 1450. Not figured.

48. *The names of vases.* The fullest catalogue of names is in the *Noms et Signes Egyptiens designant des Vases*, 1935, by Comte du Mesnil du Buisson, in which 264 names of forms are discussed. This should be used for any fresh study. They are largely of pottery forms. The better-known names of 60 stone vase forms are here listed, but the conventional figures are few of them representative, and the evidence of the use, or of Semitic names, is desirable. Another difficulty is that many are named only on the latest monuments, when the writing was corrupt, and probably the real forms were forgotten. Some help can be gained from comparison with Hebrew names, when forms were imported from Syria. The origin of the name of a vase can sometimes be traced in Egyptian or Hebrew, thus indicating for what purpose and of what size it was. Generally it may be taken that most flat-bottomed forms were of metal, and round-bottomed of stone or pottery. The names are placed in alphabetical order on pl. xlv, and numbered. The connections are placed after the names, and the identification with known forms at the end of the line. The sources followed here are Brugsch's and Erman's Dictionaries and the facsimile drawings of tombs of *Saqqara Mastabas* and of *Medum*.

Pl. XLV. 1. *Åoot*, a liquid measure, medical.

2. (Buisson, p. 44.) *Apt*, a cup, is evidently the *apt*, $\frac{1}{8}$ of the *hen*, or $9\frac{1}{2}$ cubic inches. The standard of the *hen* was rather less than a pint, so this would be a small cup. Besides this there was the large *apt* measure of 40 henu, or 1,168 cubic inches, and this name is equivalent to the Hebrew ephah of 2,300 cubic inches, double of the Egyptian standard.

3. (B. 93.) *Annure, Ynnure.* This is evidently a Syrian word; the form is an attempt to give some sound not regular in Egyptian.

4. *Anemti*, used for milk. This is from *anem*, a skin, and would be therefore the goat-skin commonly used for churning milk in Egypt. A vase might be called after that as a unit of capacity, much as a chaldron measure is named from the quantity, which is designated from a cauldron. The *anemti* would be 100 to 200 cubic inches.

5. *Anhet*, literally a "stone vase," and therefore probably not over 50 cubic inches.

6. (B. 50.) *Akană*, a two-handled jar "of Syrian work," not therefore a type found in Egypt.

7. (B. 76.) *Aken* is perhaps the same, see Hebrew *agn*, cup.

8. (B. 57.) *Ou*, a vase, and also a measure of 16 cubic inches. This is about as much as can be held in the two hands, agreeing with the measure being named from the hand. This size shows that the vase cannot be the large copper washing bowl of that form, but a smaller size which is usually of stone.

9. (B. 6.) *Onz.* This is a large bowl, by the figure. It is tempting to take the name as a derivative of *nez*, to grind; the *åyu* is often found as a

prefix, e.g. *pay*, a bird; *opy*, to play; *nem*, small; *onem*, precious stone, smallest object; *shab*, food; *oshebu*, to consume. The Egyptian commonly uses any stout bowl or pot to grind in, and a big stone bowl would be all he wants for a mortar.

10. (B. 26.) *Osh*, a beer jug, from *ash*, to pour.

11. (B. 53.) *Usheb*, a lotus cup in some texts, a situla with a hoop handle elsewhere (see *Rev. Archéol.*, 1906, i, 55).

12. (B. 30.) *Ushem*, from *shemem*, to water, probably a large pot, such as that used for sprinkling (Petrie, *Amarna*, v) or for irrigating (Wilk., *M. and C.*, fig. 144).

13. (B. 106.) *Uzu, uzeh, udeh*, a vase used in offerings; *uzeh*, libation; *uzhet*, altar.

14. (B. 80.) *Bă*, the later form of cylinder jar with hollowed sides.

15. *Pena*, the spouted jar of copper used for washing, as figured on the slate of Narmer, and in the tomb of Sekerkho-bau (*Saqq. Mast.* II, i).

16. *Mor*, apparently the Syrian measure *maris*. This probably means only a standard measure of any kind, as the Arabic *màiar*, or *àiar*; an ancient word apparently belonging to Hebrew *ȧir*, a city, i.e. a civic standard. The *maris* was of many sizes, 92½, 925, and 1,850 cubic inches in different series, showing the name does not refer to a specific amount.

17. (B. 8.) *Ment*, probably a small vase, as the *man*, gold and silver vessels, in the Aramaic of Ezra and Daniel. A small vase.

18. (B. 8.) *Ment*; this must be a different kind of vase, as it is used to measure incense, beer, and other liquids; evidently of large size.

19. (B. 76.) *Meht*, the only vase stated to be for kohl; apparently the name of the usual kohl pot.

20. (B. 26.) *Nubti*, "the golden," therefore a small vase.

21. (B. 131.) *Nemast* or *nesast*; the form resembles the large copper jar known from the tomb of Khosekhemui; at Meydum (Rahetep) it is figured of copper and of electrum. It seems to be named from the place Nemast. *Nem*, store jug of food or drink.

22. *Nen* or *nennu*, an unguent vase, therefore small.

23. *Nenhu*, a drinking jug, see *nenuh*, drunkenness.

24. *Nesut-hetep*. This was the specific name of the flat stone plate or dish, as in the lists of offerings (see *L.D.*, ii, 69).

25. (B. 70.) *Hen*. This is the principal measure, of about 29 cubic inches. There are three similar names known as measures—the *hen*, the *hennu* of four *hen*, and the Hebrew *hin* of ten *hen*. They may have been all pronounced alike, but these spellings will serve to distinguish them. There are likewise three or four different spellings in Egypt: 25, *hn*; 26 *ḥonnu*; 27 (B. 67) *ḥn, ḥnti*. These may perhaps refer to the three different measures. The source of them all may be *hen*, a lake or pool.

28. (B. 11.) *Hăr*, connected with *har*, a basin or pool.

29. *Hut*, the form as a large metal bowl is well given by Seker-kho-bau and Rahetep. It was probably connected with *hud*, an offering.

30. (B. 115.) *Hest*. This is a very well-known form in bronze, as metal vase, fig. 68.

31. *Heti*, a heart-shaped vase, with two handles and a wide mouth.

32. *Heken*, a word meaning offering or ointment; it is apparently applied to the vase at Meydum, and seems to mean simply an offering vase; this and the other senses all coming from *heknu*, to adore.

33. *Heden*, a vase of oil.

34. (B. 65.) *Khăy*, a vase measure of ⅓ *hen*, 9½ cubic inches. It comes from *khăy*, a leather vessel; and the only pottery copied from a leather flask has in the early examples a capacity of 10 or 11 cub. ins. This fixes the form from Syria known as the *bilbil*.

35. (B. 65.) *Khăt, khăut, khăui*, the stone table for offerings, usual in the iind and iiird dynasties, being well figured with the name at Meydum, where it is said to be of alabaster, the usual material. It is connected with *khăo*, to deposit, being the place where offerings were deposited in the tomb.

36. (B. 63.) *Khebeb* or *khebkheb*. The determinatives for this word differ much. The first suggests the larger bronze basin type, drawing in upward, which belongs to about the early Greek age. Possibly this was a measure rather than a specific form, and connected with the Greek measure *khous*, which means simply a heap, and which varied from 210 to 932 cubic inches. The Egyptian would sound as *khevev*.

37. (B. 45.) *Khnem*, the well-known vase with long handle and a lifting lug in front.

38. (B. 25, 26). *Senu*, perhaps connected with the *tzintzehneth*, the pot of manna put in the ark.

39. (B. 139.) *Sery*, the Hebrew *sīr*, a cooking pot; Arabic *zīr*, a large jar; hence perhaps the Indian *sīr* measure, which is much varied in size, but usually

about 60 cubic inches ; as the determinative has two handles, it seems likely to be the usual two-handled cooking pot.

40. (B. 53.) *Seshen*, Hebrew *shushan*, a lily ; the lotus cup.

41. (B. 74.) *Seti* ; 42, *sethel*. These are variant names. On the stele of Naukratis this is rendered by *keramion*, a big jar, stated by Brugsch at 1,610 cubic inches. There might otherwise be a connection between the *seti* and the Syrian *saton* of 740 cubic inches. Seeing how often the same name is used for a measure and its double, both of these connections may be true. The Egyptian pot was certainly large, as *sethel* means brewing.

43. *Shădu*, is probably connected with *shat*, wine.

44. *Shamu* or *Aăkhet* is a large jar, probably connected with the idea of the inundation. It is placed on a stand, pierced with triangular holes, which was usual in the Old Kingdom, made of stone or of pottery.

45. *Shauabti*, probably a wooden measure made of *shauabu*, persea wood.

46. (B. 85.) *Shedy*, a brewing jar, from *shed*, brewing ; therefore large.

47. *Qărnebu*, of silver. Probably a horn-shaped vase, from Hebrew *qeren*, horn.

48. (B. 29.) *Qeb*, a small vessel for lamp oil ; Hebrew *qab*, 128 cubic inches.

49. (B. 111.) *Qebh*, a libation vase with a spout, from *qebh*, coolness.

50. (B. 62.) *Qerer* or *qelel*, Hebrew *kelī*, a vessel (common throughout O.T.) ; Arabic *qulleh*, water jar. From the last it may be the long tubular drinking pot used in the Empire.

51. *Ka-hen*, " servant of the *ka*," the name of the *ka*-priest, here applied to a pot for drink which ministers to the *ka*. Compare a small poker called a " curate."

52. (B. 72.) *Găy*, a liquid measure, from *gă*, liquid.

53. *Tenau*, a flat dish, see *tennu*, largeness.

54. *Tennu*, a large vessel, *tennu*, largeness, quantity. Probably the hand-washing bowl of the early dynasties.

55. *Tet*, a large open vessel, see Hebrew *dud*, cauldron, pot.

56. (B. 64.) *Thebu*, a metal jug, measure, probably not large. Perhaps connected with *tebă*, *zebo*, digit, so a fraction of a larger measure, as the digit is of a cubit.

57. *Debh* from *debhu*, an offering, an offering vase.

58. (B. 9.) *Defa*, a metal bowl with two handles, figured at Meydum, and the tomb of Seker-kho-bau. Probably *zuau*, *tuau*, a measure vase.

59. (B. 18.) *Des*, a beer jar ; compare *tesaf*, a liquid offering, *tesef*, a bread offering.

60. *Tshărbu*, a patera or drinking bowl, see Arabic *shorba*, a drink. This is probably the deep bowl (metal 41–54) used for drinking, as figured on the monuments.

INDEX

1
2
3
4
5
6
7
8
9
10
11
12
13
14
15

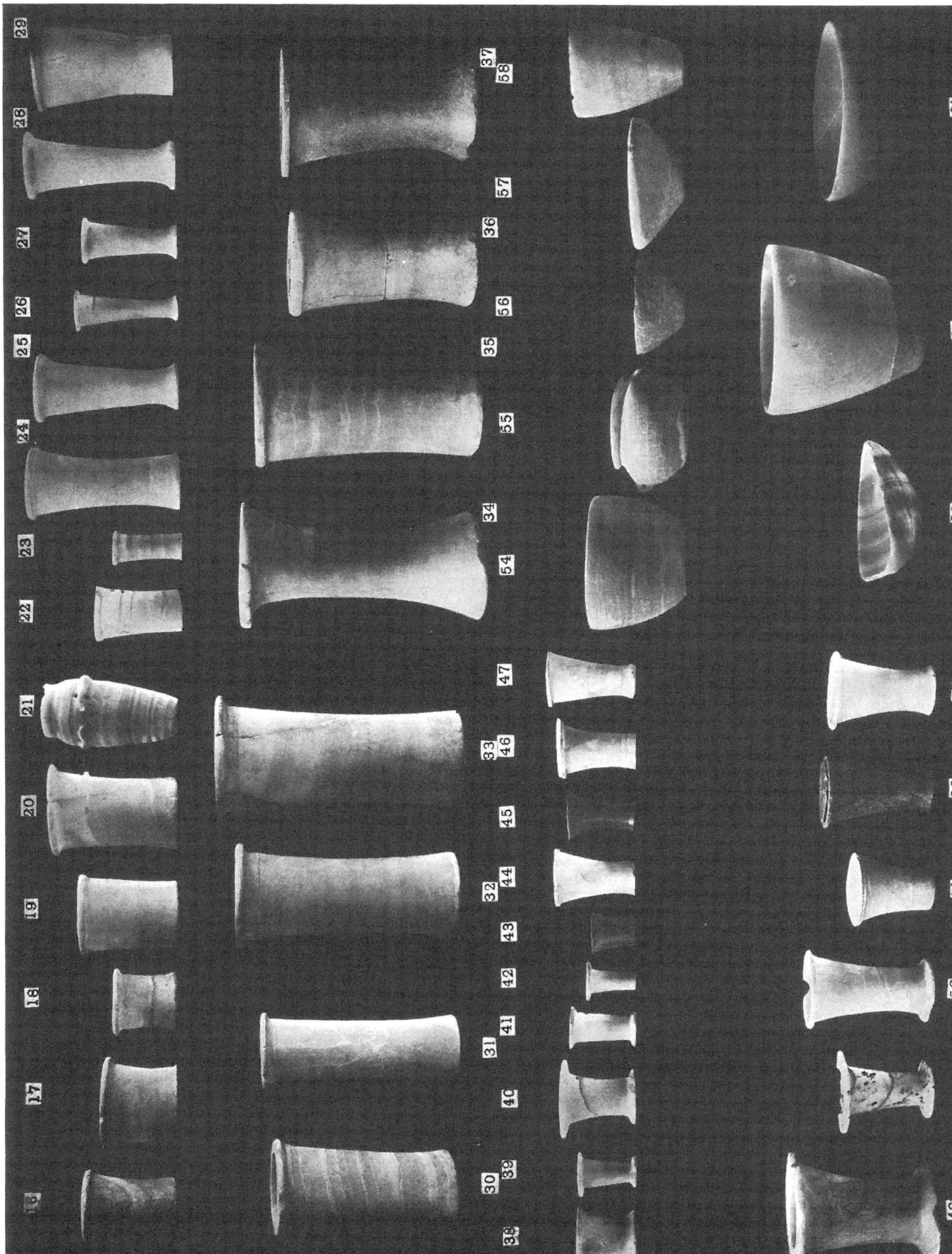

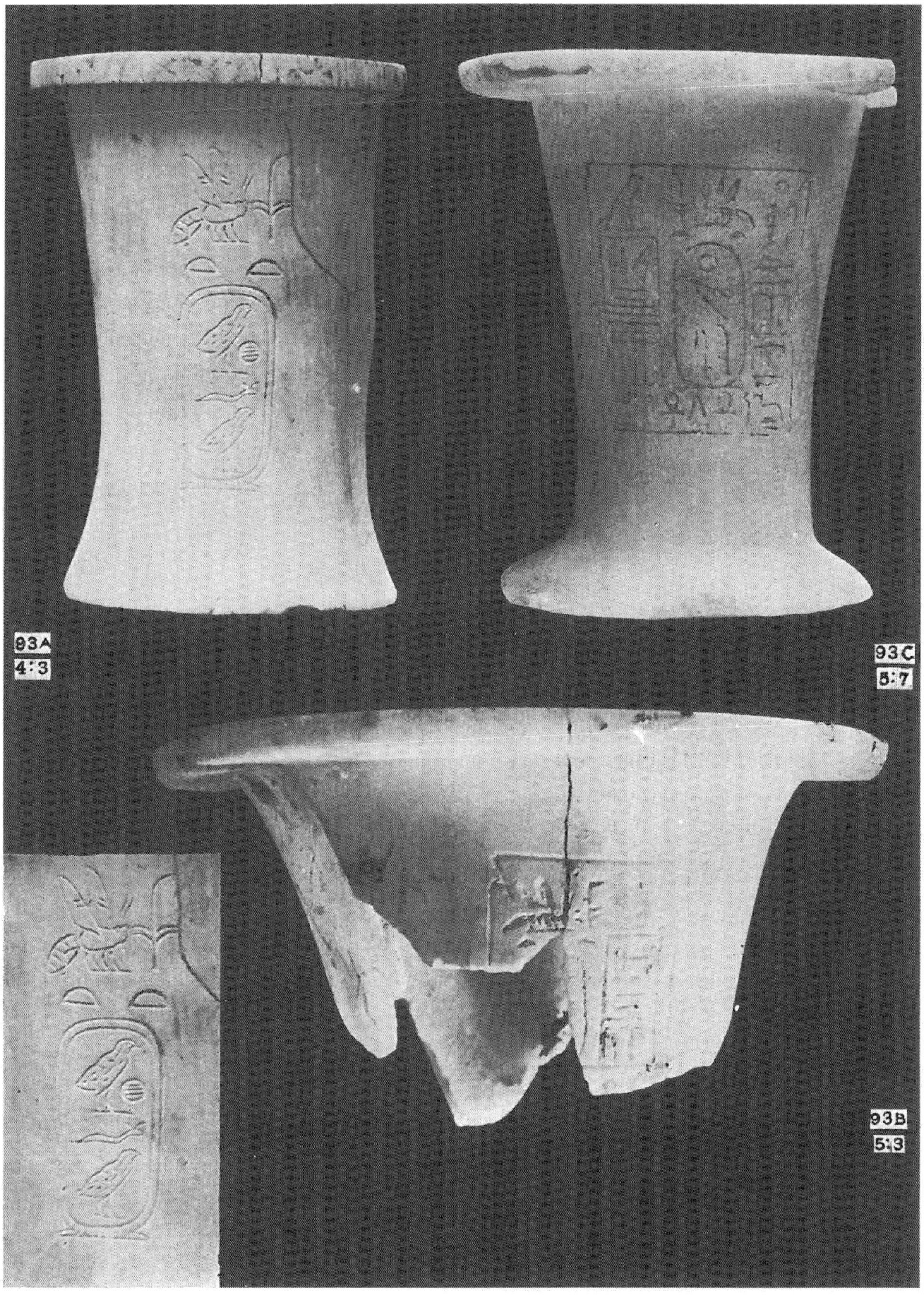

93A 4:3

93C 5:7

93B 5:3

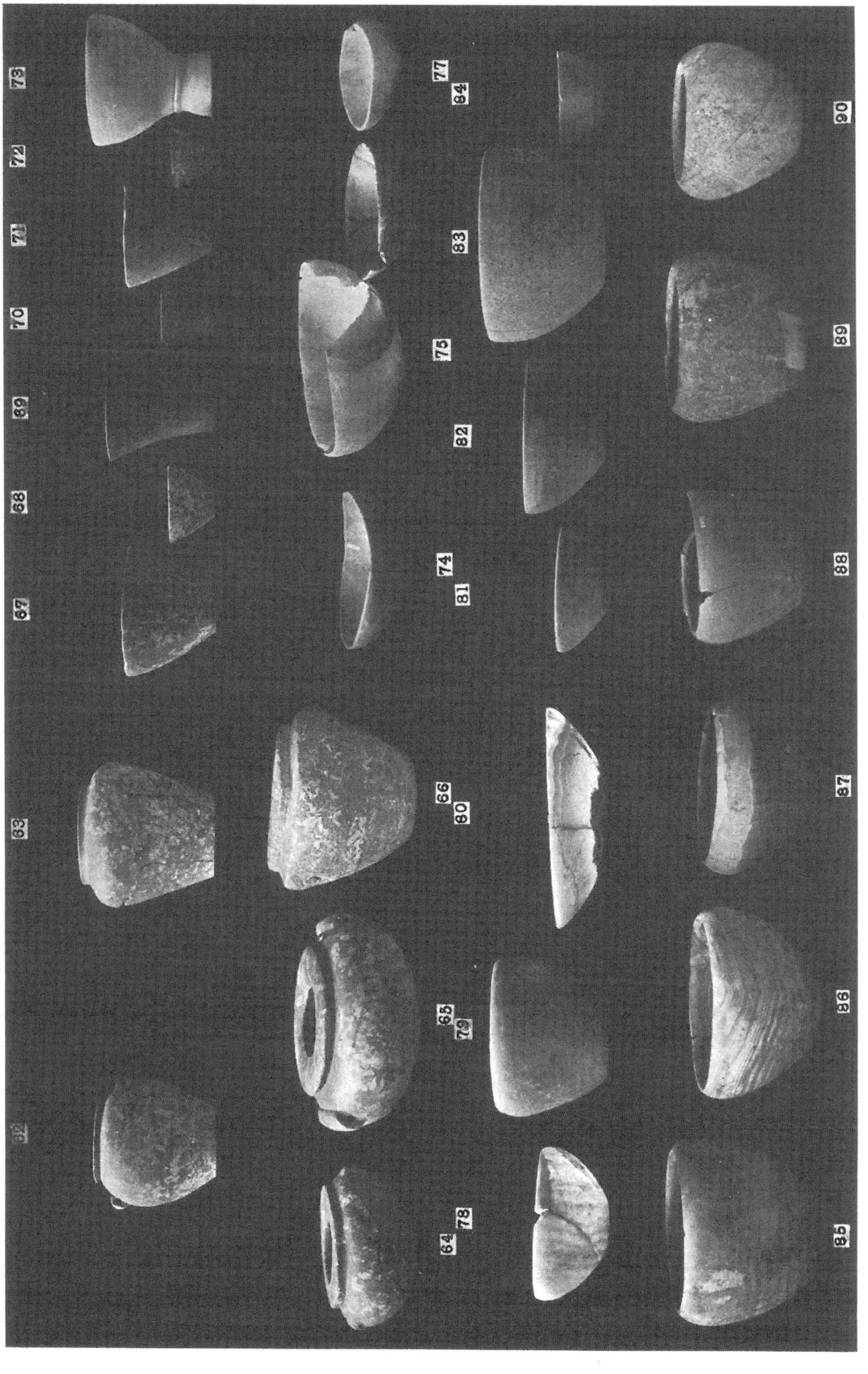
63
64
65
66
67
68
69
70
71
72
73
74
75
77
78
79
80
81
82
83
84
85
86
87
88
89
90

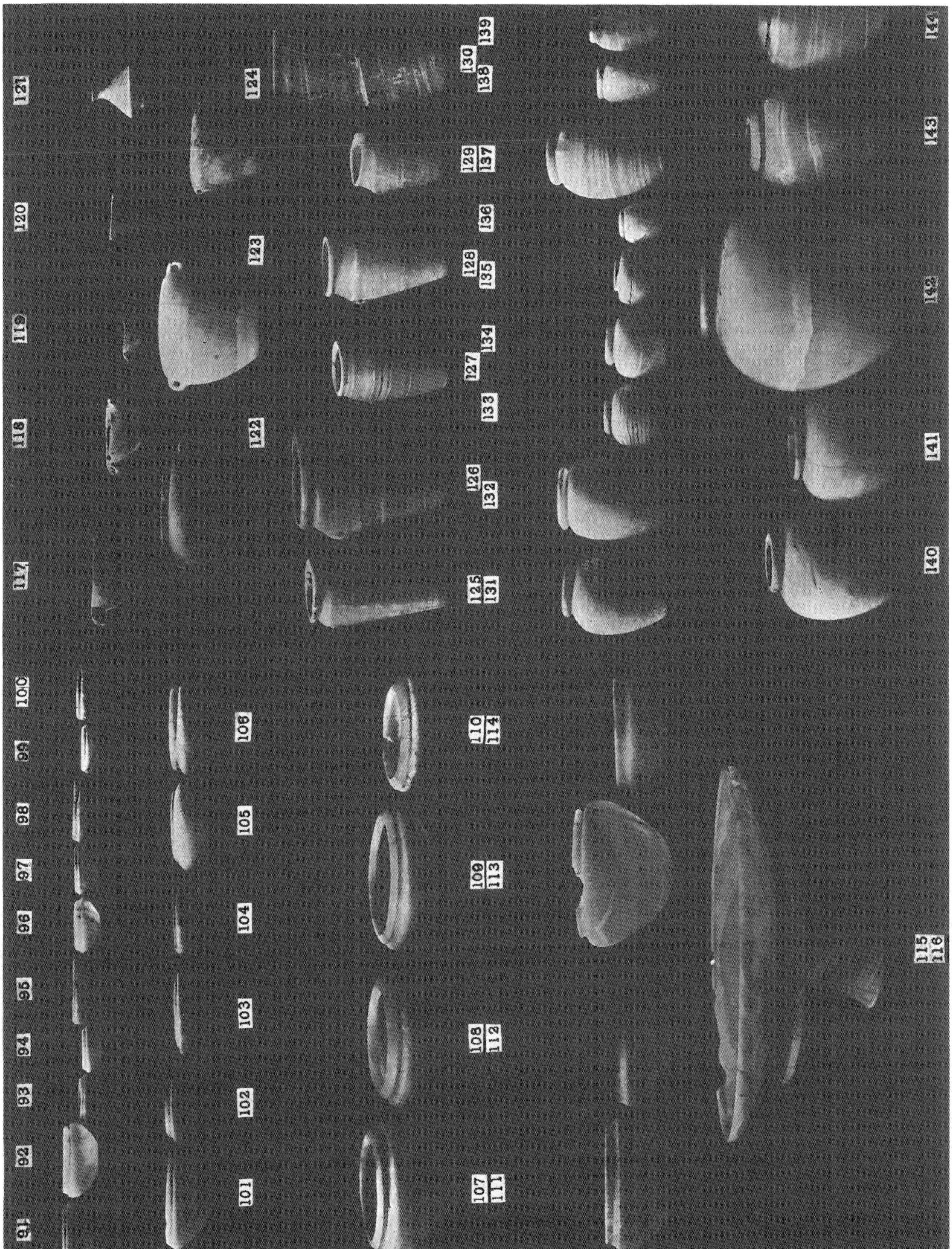
91 92 93 94 95 96 97 98 99 100
101 102 103 104 105 106
107 111 108 112 109 113 110 114
115 116
117 118 119 120 121
122 123 124
125 131 126 132 127 133 134 128 135 136 129 137 130 138 139
140 141 142 143 144

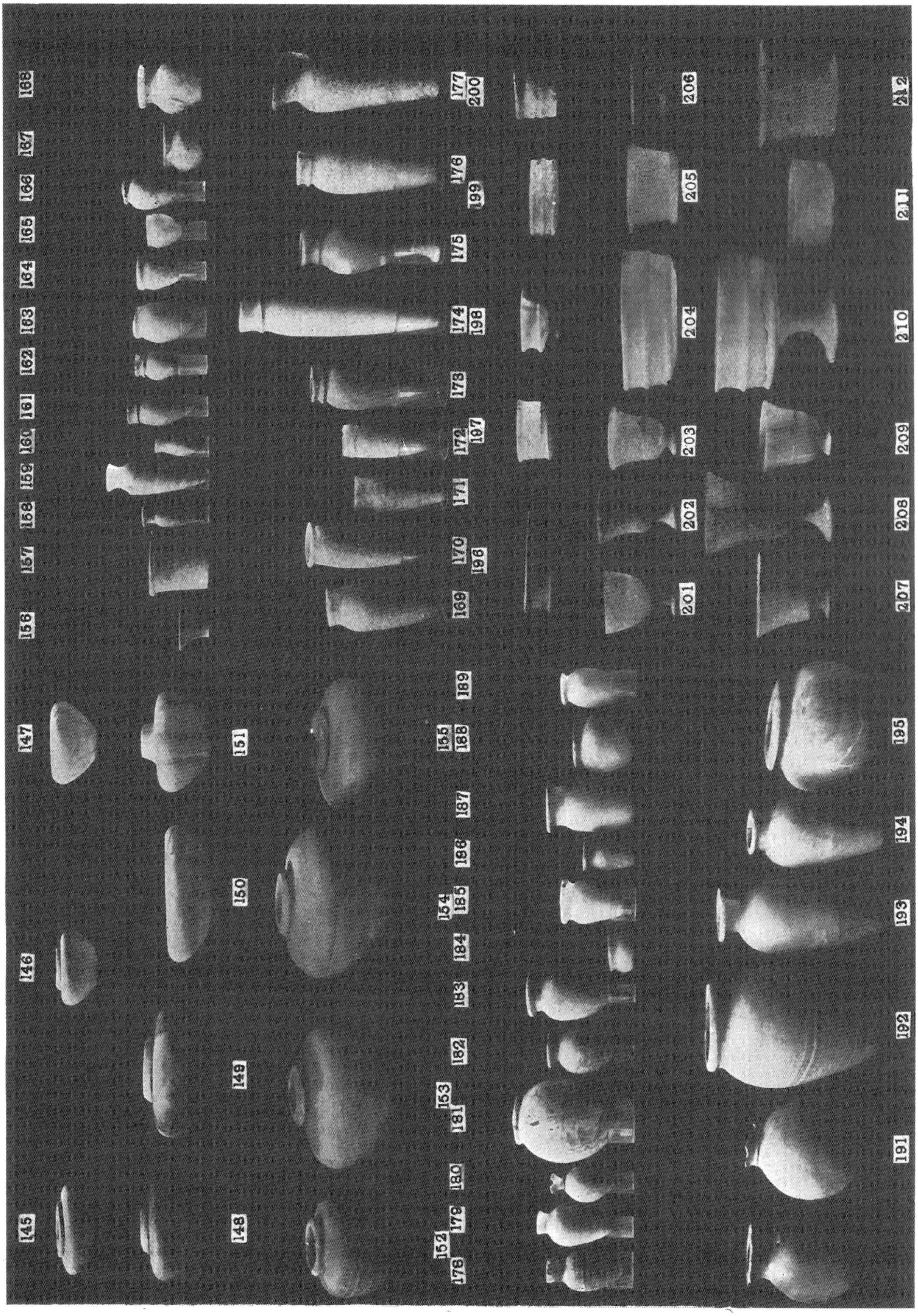

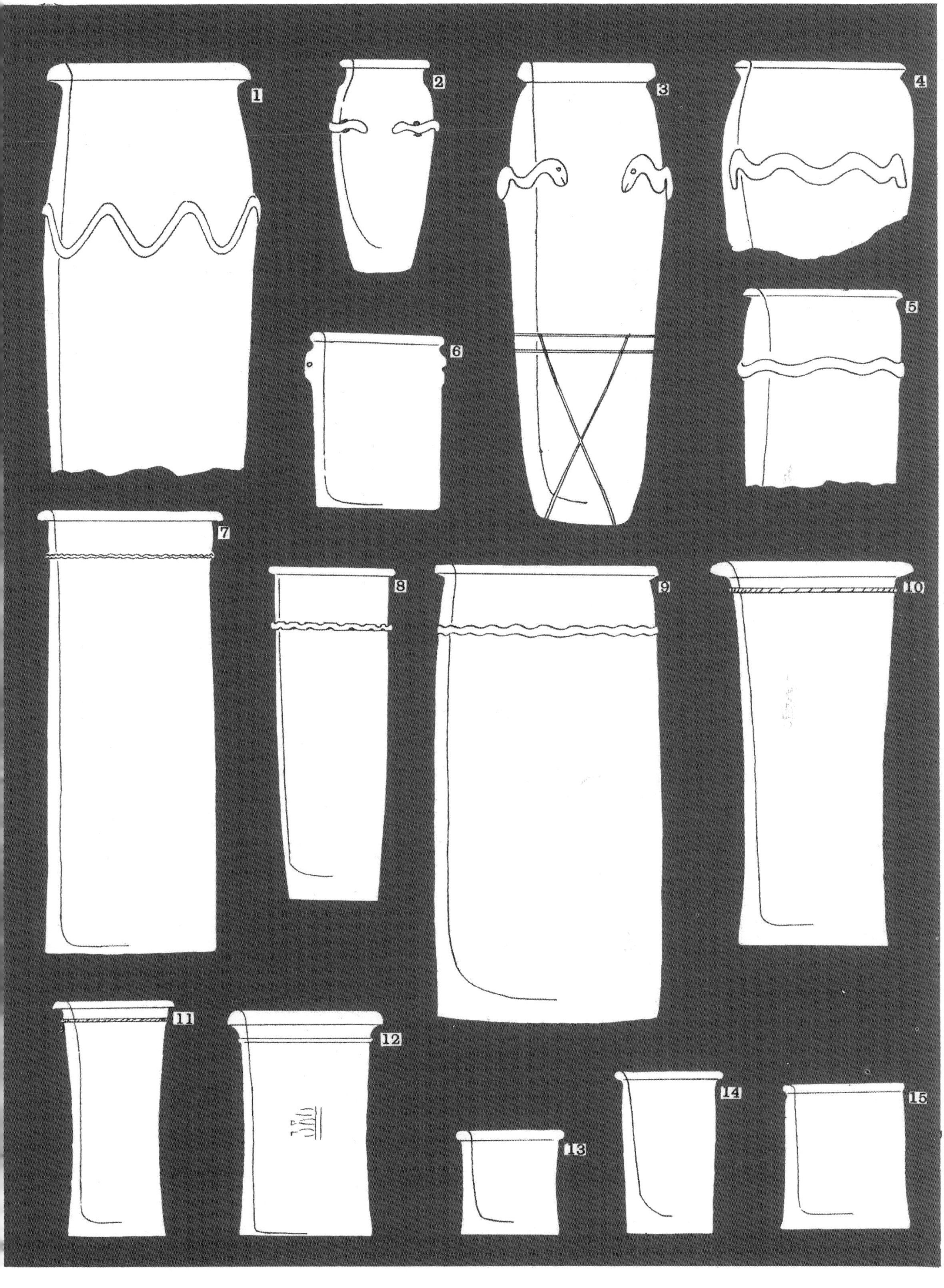
1
2
3
4
5
6
7
8
9
10
11
12
13
14
15

16
17
18
21
24
22
23
19
20
25
26
27
30
28
29

31
32
33
34
35
36
37
38
39
40
41
42
43

44
45
46
47
48
49
50
51
52
53
54
55
56
57
58
59
60
61

62
63
64
65
66
67
68
69
70
71
72
73
74
75
76

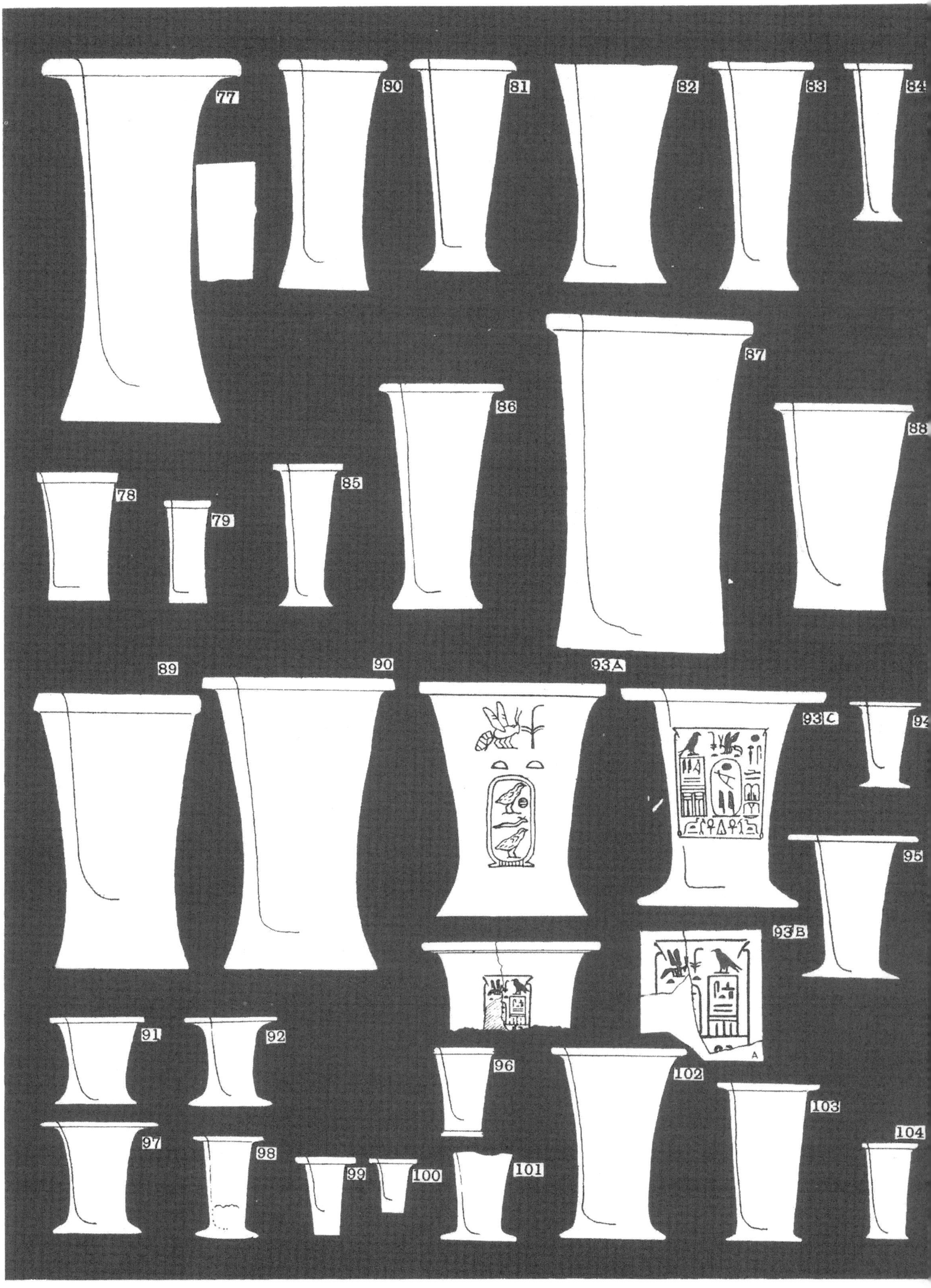
77
78
79
80
81
82
83
84
85
86
87
88
89
90
91
92
93A
93B
93C
94
95
96
97
98
99
100
101
102
103
104

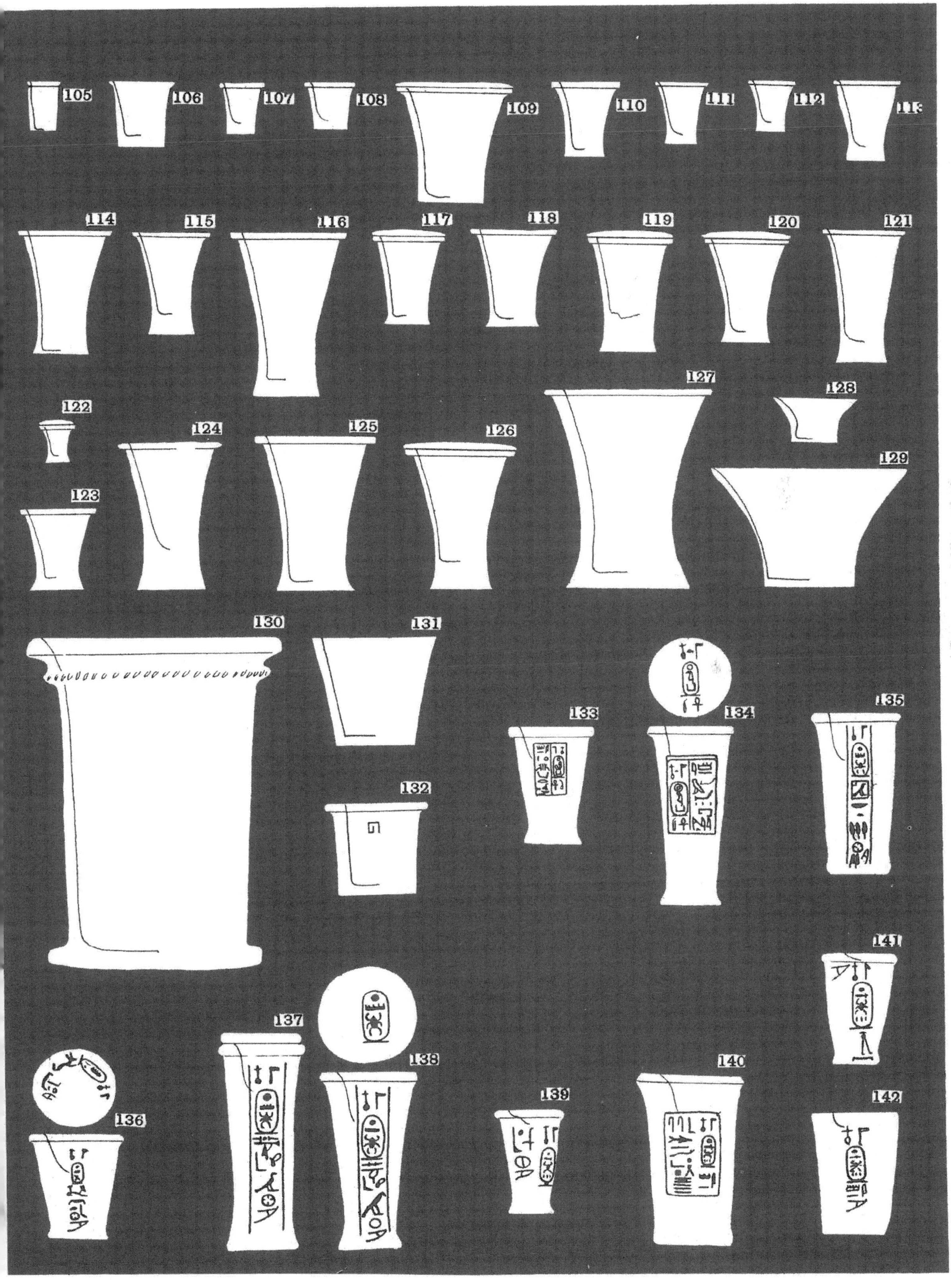
105
106
107
108
109
110
111
112
113
114
115
116
117
118
119
120
121
122
123
124
125
126
127
128
129
130
131
132
133
134
135
136
137
138
139
140
141
142

BRIMS	A	B	C	D	E	F	G	H	J	K	L
S.D. 77	2										
78	8	5									
B 79	10	4									
O 79	22	9									
80	44	25									
81	38	29	1								
82	16	5	1								
NETEREN	2										
PERABSN											
II LATE			1	14							
III EARLY	2	3	1		1	1					
III LATE											
V–VI		1				4	4		2		
IX						1		1			
XI						1					
XII											
										9 + 12	+ 9

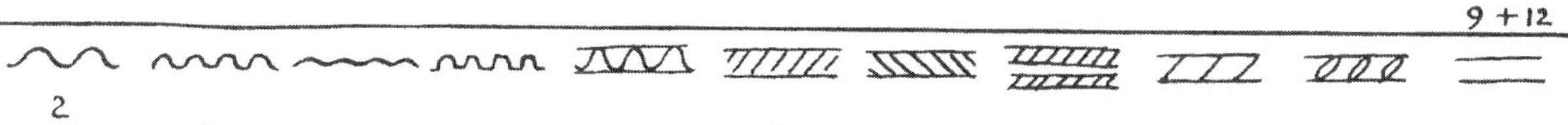

BANDS												NONE
S.D. 77	2											
78	4	2				3		1				2
B 79	1	1	4		1	5				2		2
O 79				1		10			2	1	4	5
80		1	4	1		39	2	1	6		7	9
81	3		2			11	1	1	6	1	16	19
82						4			3	7	2	3
NETEREN												2
PERABSEN												
II LATE												14
III EARLY						2						37
III LATE												
V–VI												16
IX												5
XI												2
XII												
												9 + 21

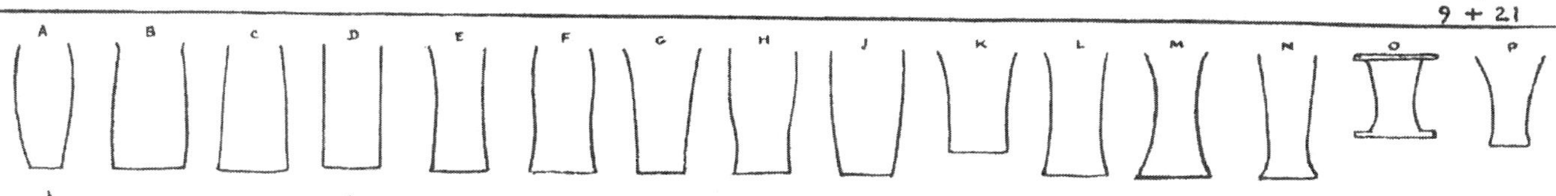

SIDES	A	B	C	D	E	F	G	H	J	K	L	M	N	O	P
77	1			2											
78	1	4		4	1										
B 79	1		1	1	1										
O 79			5	5	7	1	1		1	1	3				
80		1	2	12	26		1		1	1	9				
81		3	1	11	24		2		1	7	17	1			
82				1	2						1	2	1		
NETEREN					1						1	1			
PERABSEN															
II LATE				1					1	10	2				
III EARLY					10		1	2			2	2	1		
III LATE													1		
V–VI												1	8	1	
IX														2	
XI														1	
XII														1	
															8 + 21

BOWLS	BRIM										IN BASE			
77		3												1
78	8	5										1	1	16
B 79	4	1	1	1	1						5			
O 79	12	11	6	7	1						10	8	4	2
80	22	12	15	38	6			3	1		13	26		3
Y 81	3	3		7	3			1			2	5		1
T 81	5	5	4	14	1	3	4	1			5	21		3
X 81		1		1	1						1	1	1	
82	14	12	1	28		11	12	3	2	1	15	32	7	9
NET' 'EN						5	11		3	1	3	4	1	6
PER SEN	14	2	1	1			6		1		3		1	3
II ATE						1	2						1	2
III ARLY	5	8	9	2		8	19	8	2	2				54
III LATE		3				2	9			1		2	1	10
IY- VI				1										4

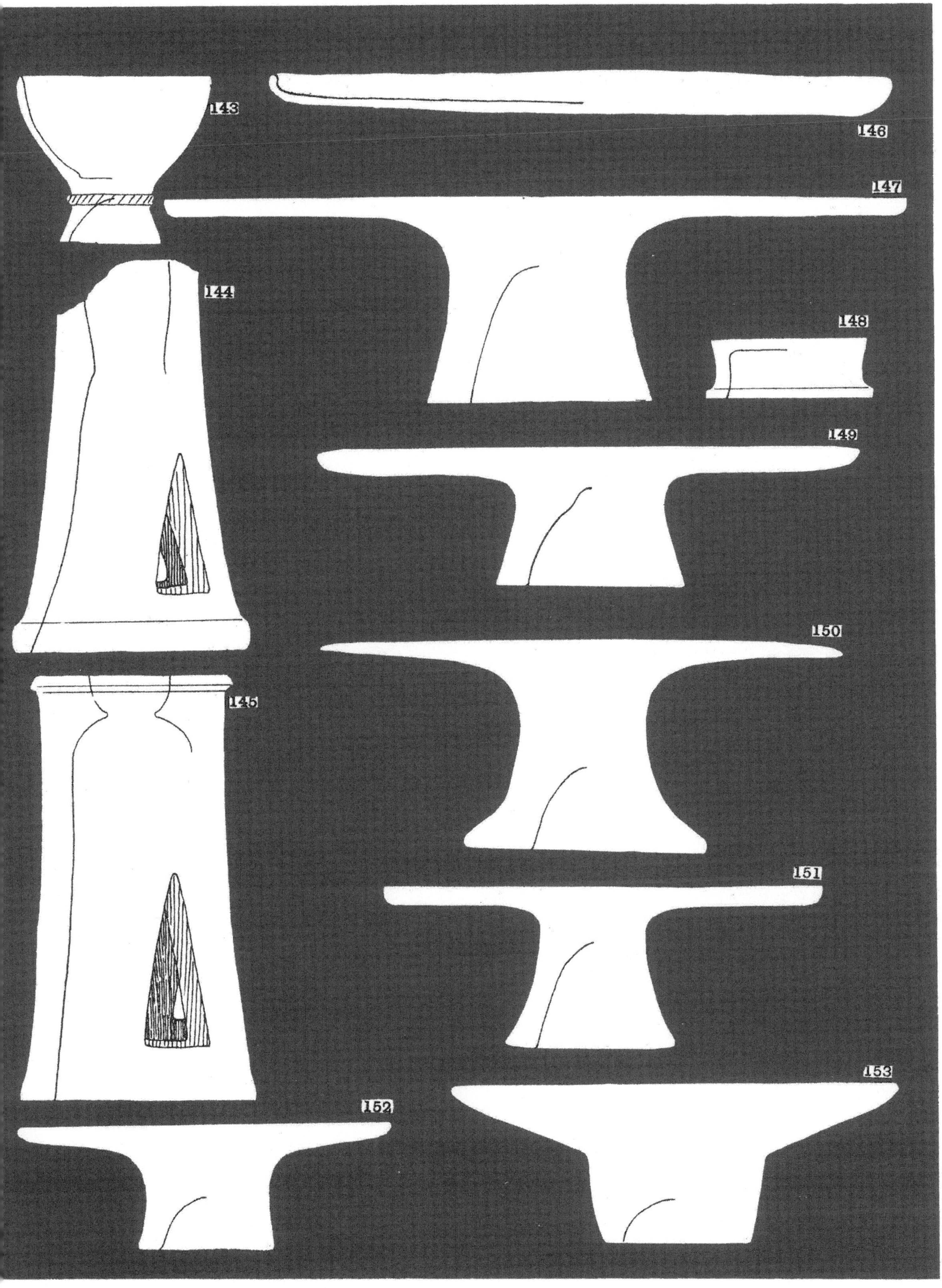
143
144
145
146
147
148
149
150
151
152
153

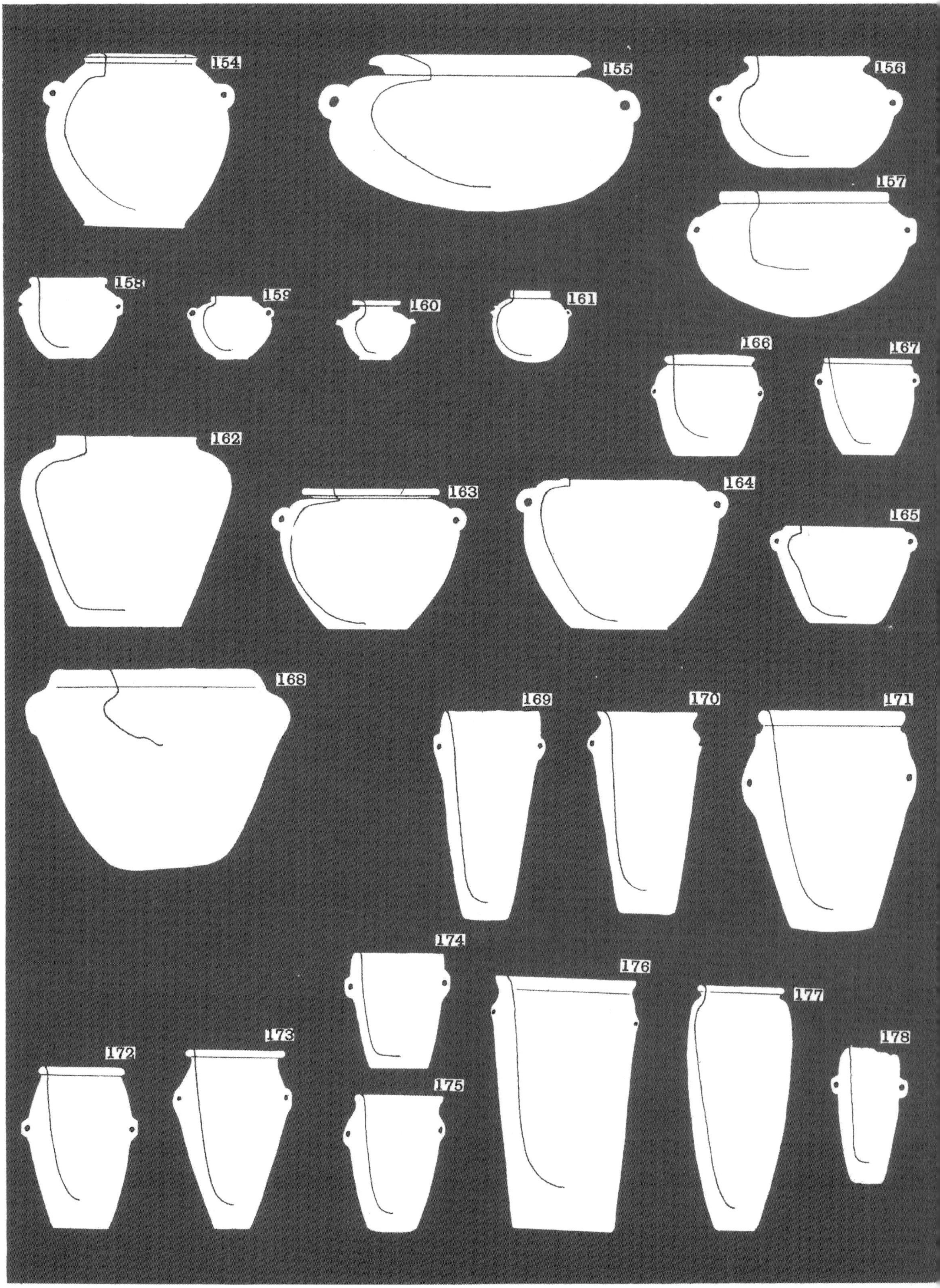
154
155
156
157
158
159
160
161
166
167
162
163
164
165
168
169
170
171
174
176
177
173
172
175
178

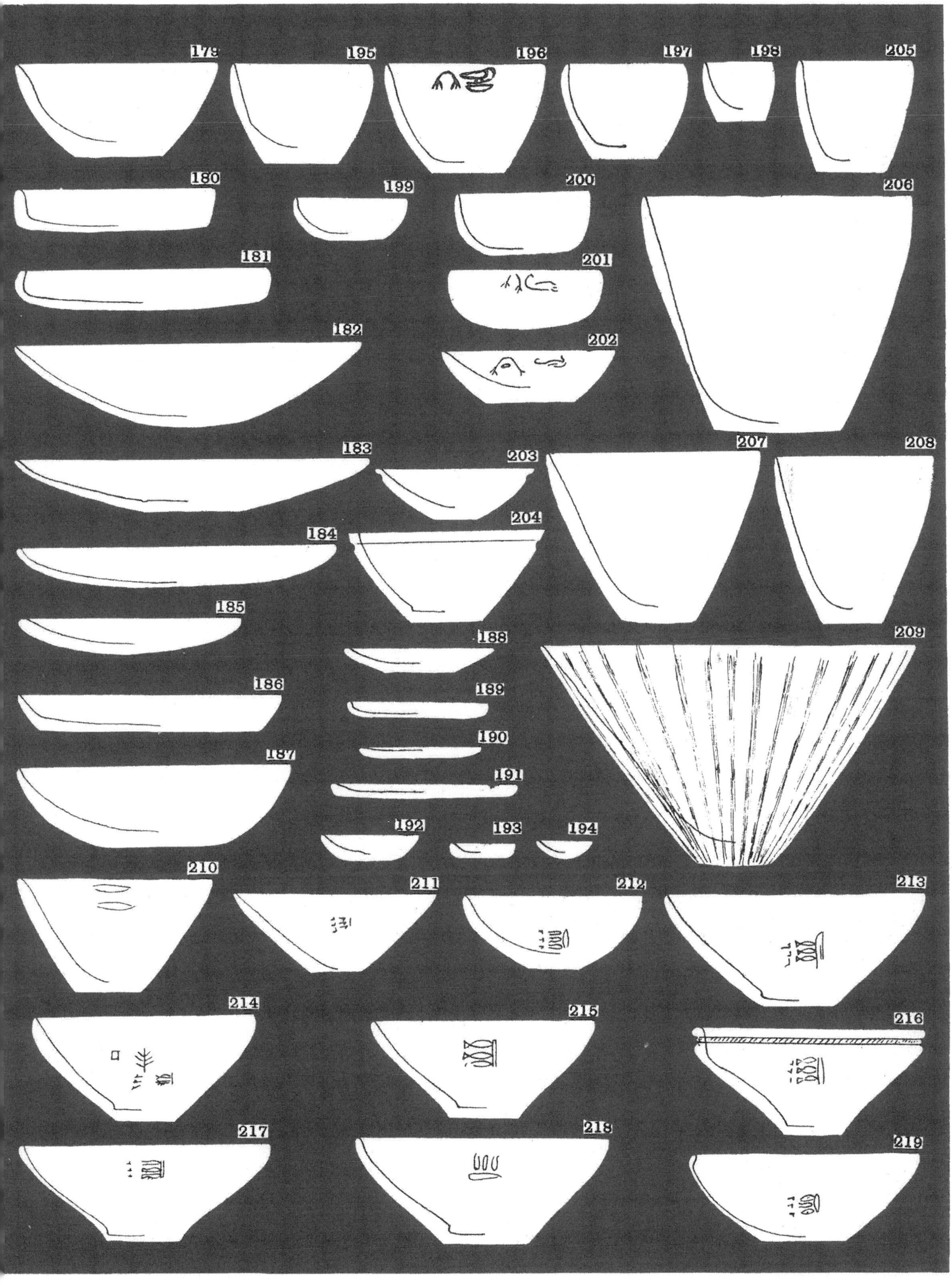
179
195
196
197
198
205
180
199
200
206
181
201
182
202
183
203
207
208
184
204
185
188
209
186
189
190
187
191
192
193
194
210
211
212
213
214
215
216
217
218
219

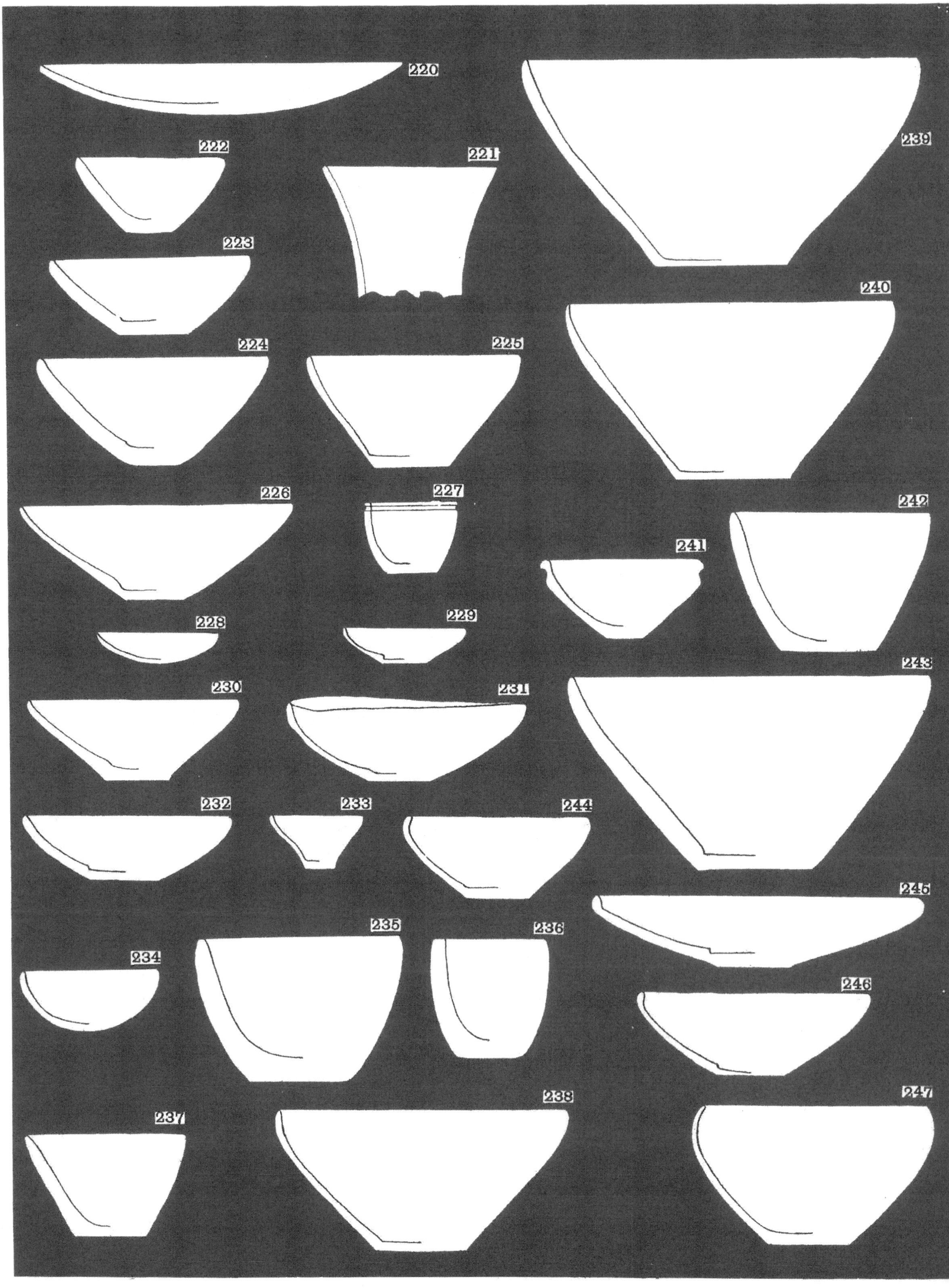
220
239
222
221
223
240
224
225
226
227
242
241
228
229
243
230
231
232
233
244
245
235
236
234
246
238
247
237

248
249
250
251
252
253
254
255
256
257
258
259
260
261
262
263
264
265
266
267
268
269
270
271
272
273
274
275
276
277

278
279
280
281
282
283
284
285
286
287
288
289
290
291
292
299
293
294
300
295
296
301
297
303
302
298

304
309
310
305
311
306
313
312
307
308
319
314
320
322
321
315
323
316
325
324
317
326
318
327
328

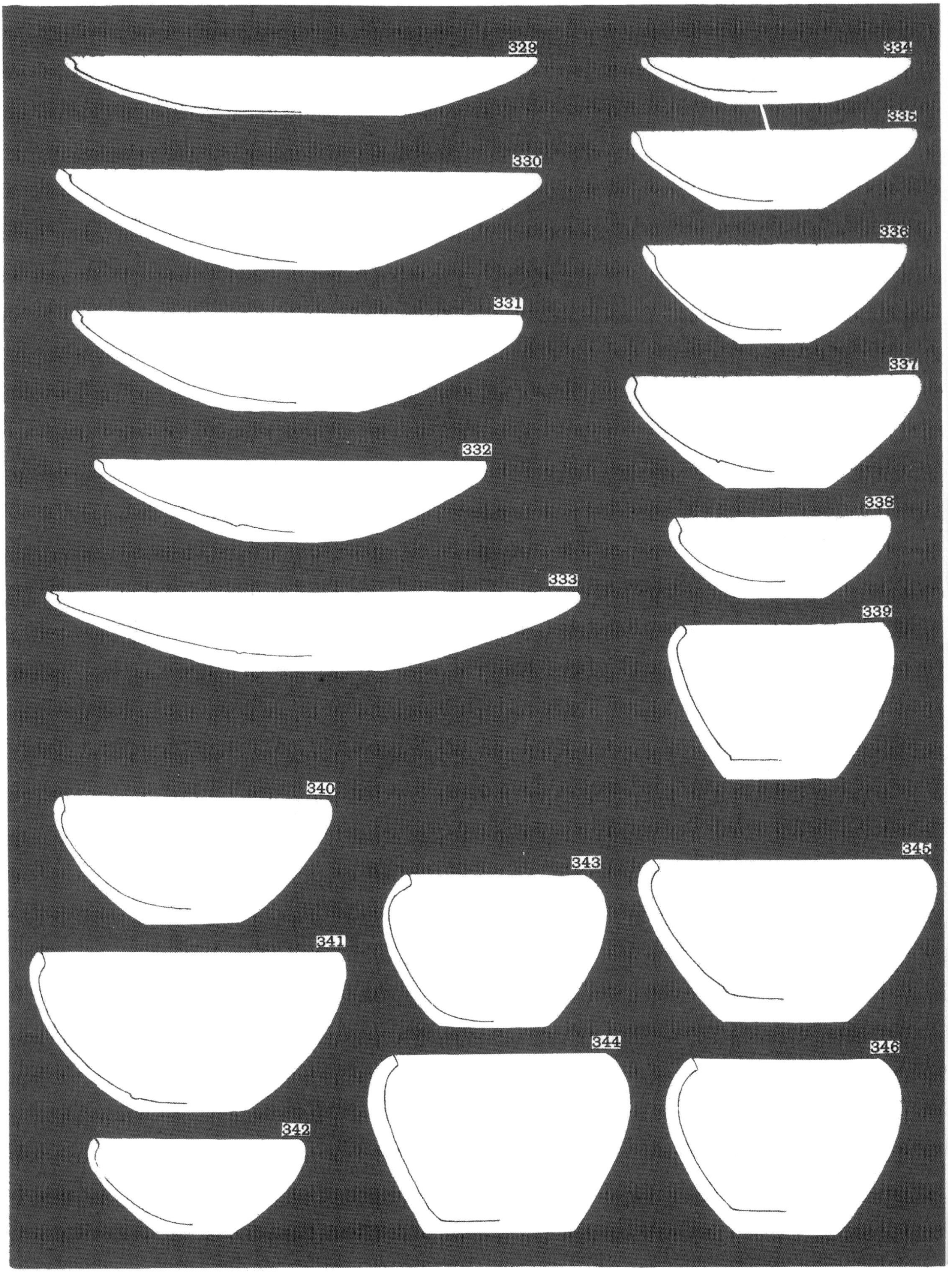
329
330
331
332
333
334
335
336
337
338
339
340
341
342
343
344
345
346

347
348
359
349
350
357
360
358
351
361
362
352
363
353
365
354
364
366
355
367
371
368
356
370
369

372
373
374
375
376
377
378
379
380
381
382
383
384
385
386
387
388
389
390
391
392
393
394
395
396

397
398
403
404
407
399
400
405
408
409
401
402
406
410
411
413
414
415
412
416
417
418
419
420
421
422
423
424
425
426
427
428
429
430
433
431
432
434
435
436
437
439
440
441
442
443
438
444
445
446
447
448

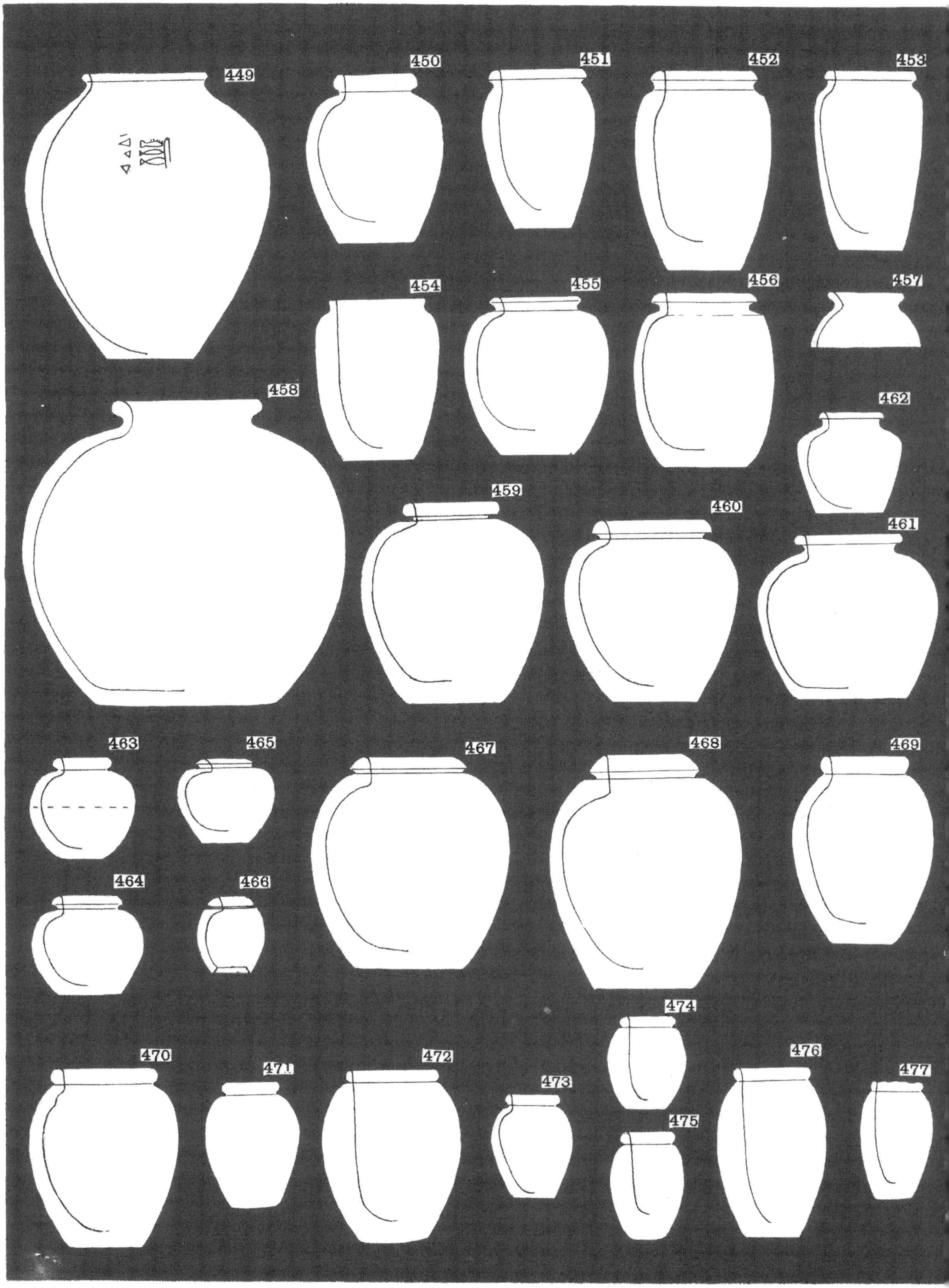
449
450
451
452
453
454
455
456
457
458
459
460
461
462
463
464
465
466
467
468
469
470
471
472
473
474
475
476
477

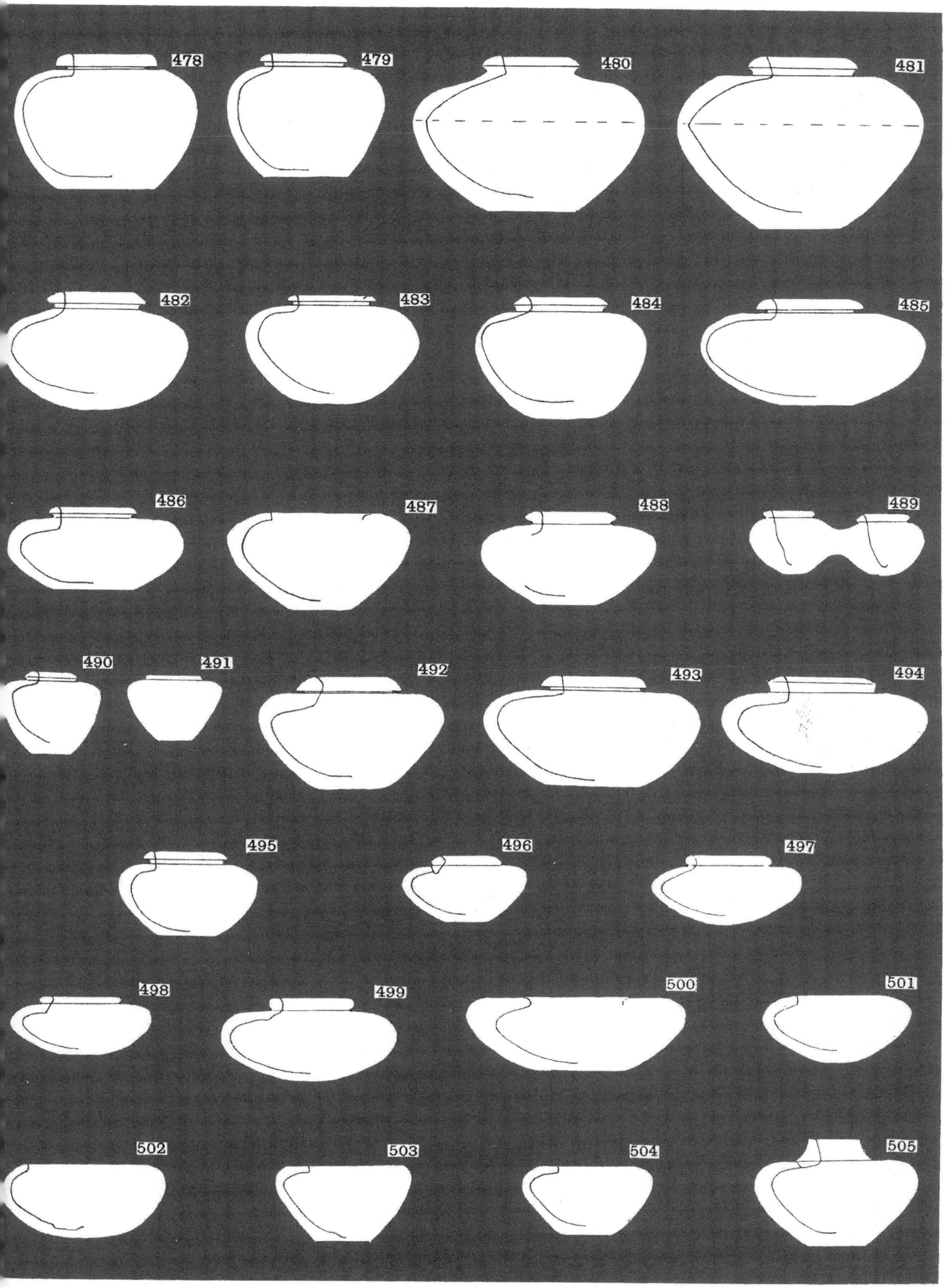
478
479
480
481
482
483
484
485
486
487
488
489
490
491
492
493
494
495
496
497
498
499
500
501
502
503
504
505

506
507
508
509
511
512
513
514
515
516
517
510
518
519
520
521
522
523
524
525
526
527
528
529
530
531
532
533
534
53
536
537
538
539
541
540
547
542
544
543
548
545
546
549

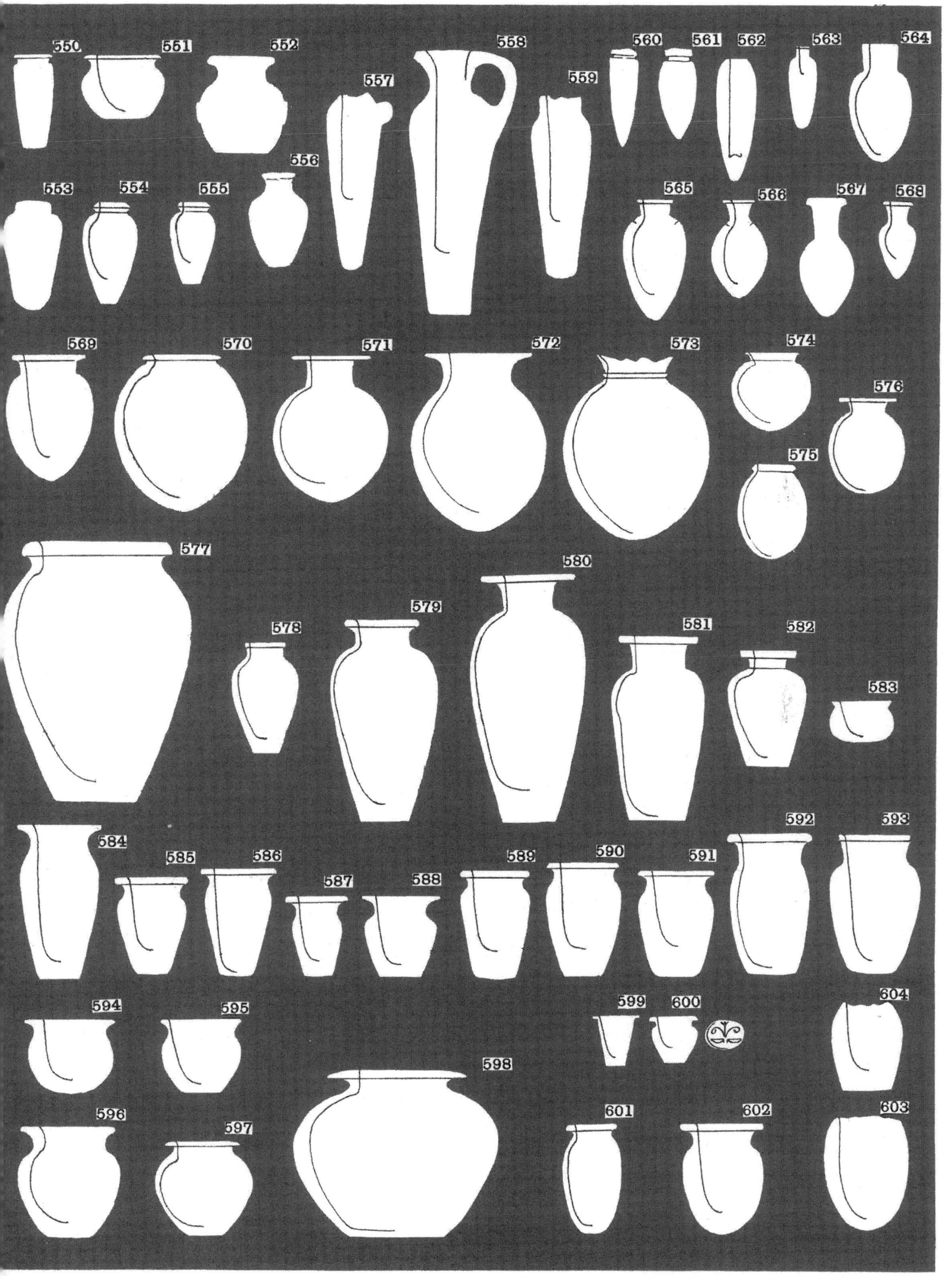
550
551
552
553
554
555
556
557
558
559
560
561
562
563
564
565
566
567
568
569
570
571
572
573
574
575
576
577
578
579
580
581
582
583
584
585
586
587
588
589
590
591
592
593
594
595
596
597
598
599
600
601
602
603
604

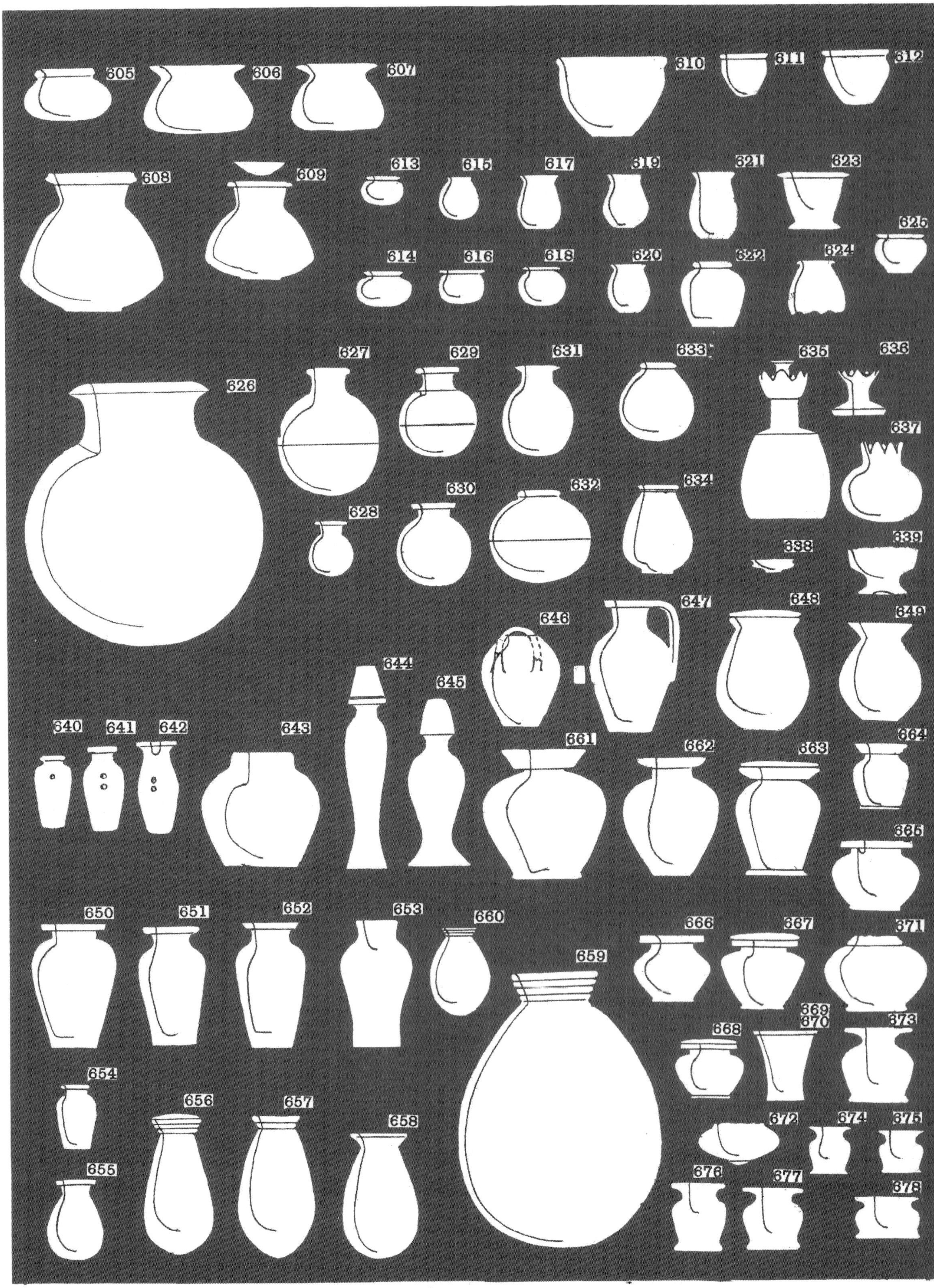
605
606
607
610
611
612
608
609
613
615
617
619
621
623
625
614
616
618
620
622
624
626
627
629
631
633
635
636
637
628
630
632
634
638
639
646
647
648
649
644
645
640
641
642
643
661
662
663
664
665
650
651
652
653
660
659
666
667
671
668
669
670
673
654
656
657
658
655
672
674
675
676
677
678

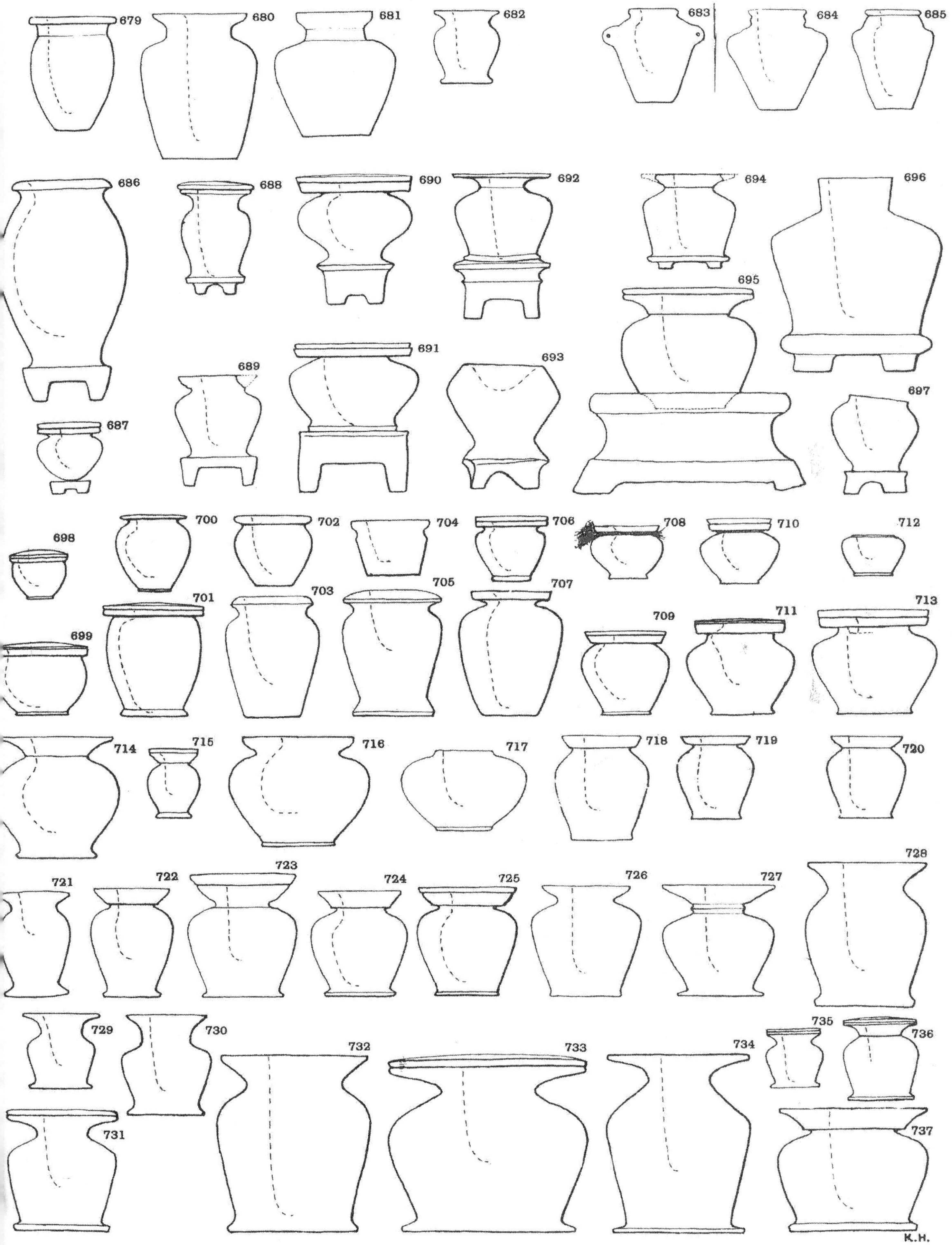
679 680 681 682 683 684 685
686 688 690 692 694 696
695
689 691 693
687 697
698 700 702 704 706 708 710 712
701 703 705 707 709 711 713
699
714 715 716 717 718 719 720
721 722 723 724 725 726 727 728
729 730 732 733 734 735 736
731 737
K.H.

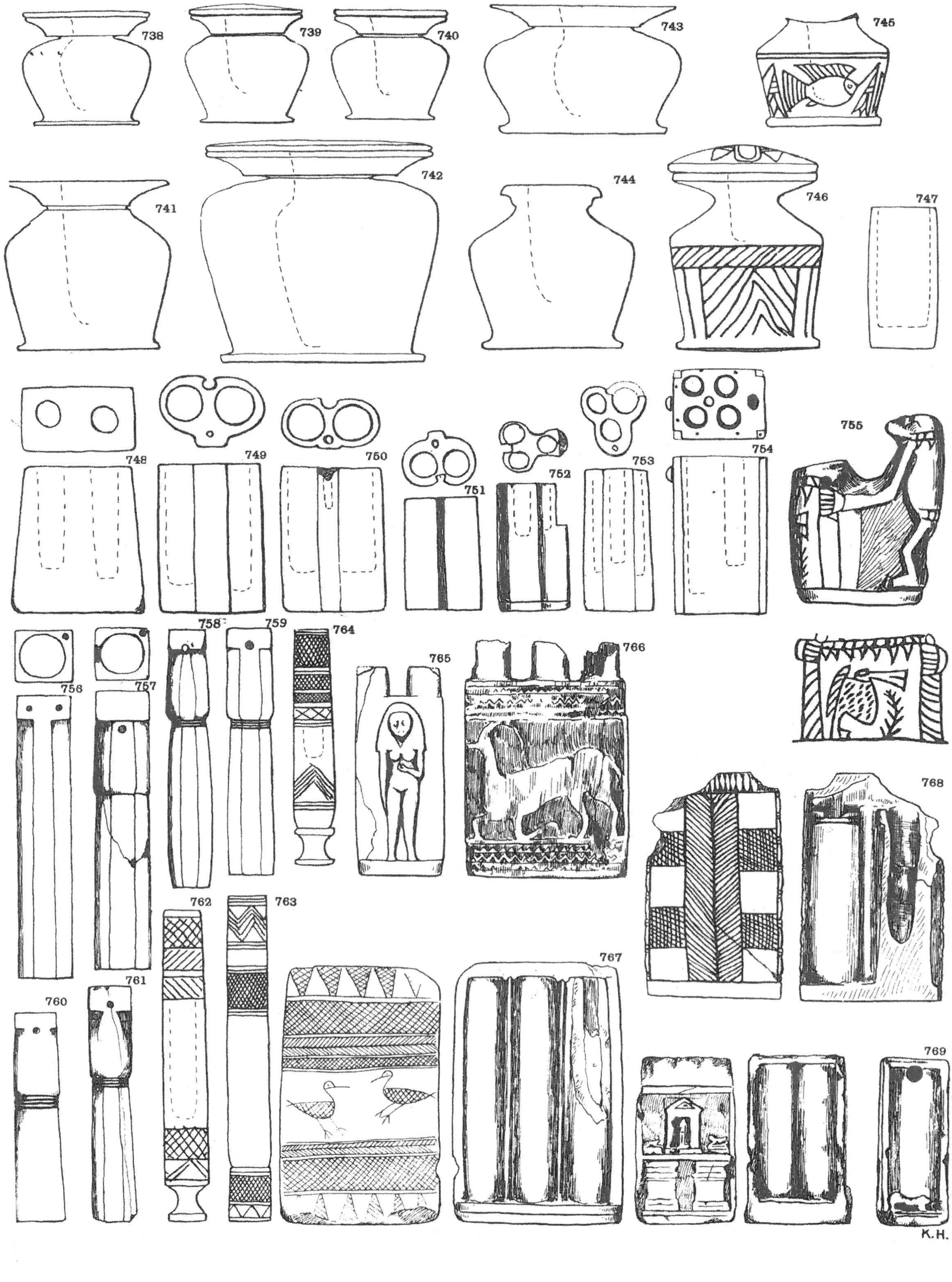
738
739
740
743
745
741
742
744
746
747
748
749
750
751
752
753
754
755
756
757
758
759
764
765
766
768
762
763
760
761
767
769
K.H.

770
771
772
773
774
775
776
777
778
779
780
781
782
783
784
785
786
787
788
789
790
791
792
793
794
795
796
797
798
799
800
801
802
803
804
805
806
807
755
808
809
810
811
812
813
814
815
816
817
818
819

820
821
822
823
824
825
826
827
828
829
830
831
832
833
834
835
836
837
838
839
840
841
842
843
844
845
846
847
848
849
850
851
852
853
854
855
856
857
858
859

860
862
863
864
865
866
861
869
870
871
872
868
867
873
875
877
878
880
881
876
874
879
882
883
884
885

886
887
888
889
890
891
892
893
894
895
896
897
898
899
900
901
902
903
904
905
906
907
908
909
910
911
912
913
914

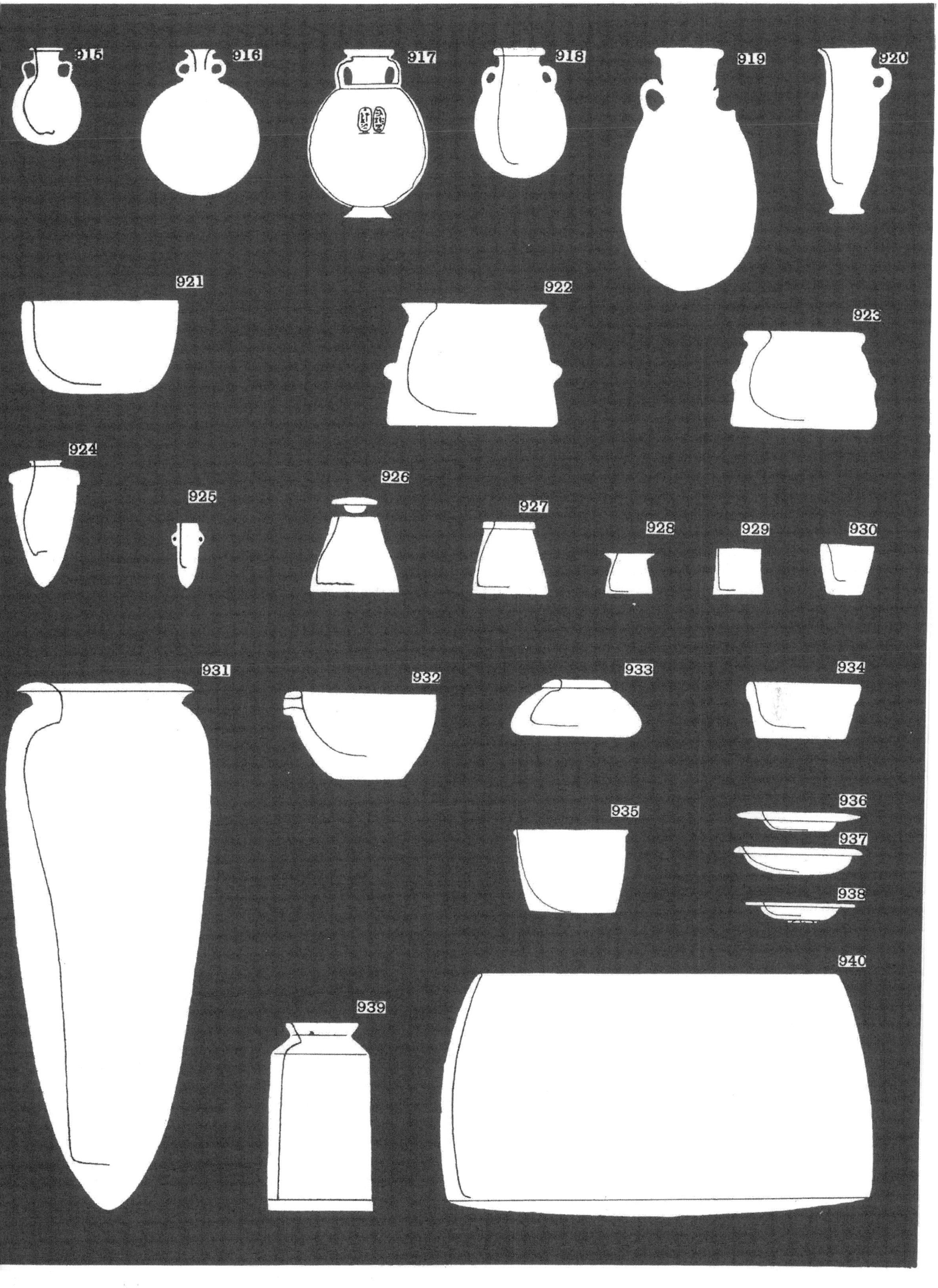
915
916
917
918
919
920
921
922
923
924
925
926
927
928
929
930
931
932
933
934
935
936
937
938
939
940

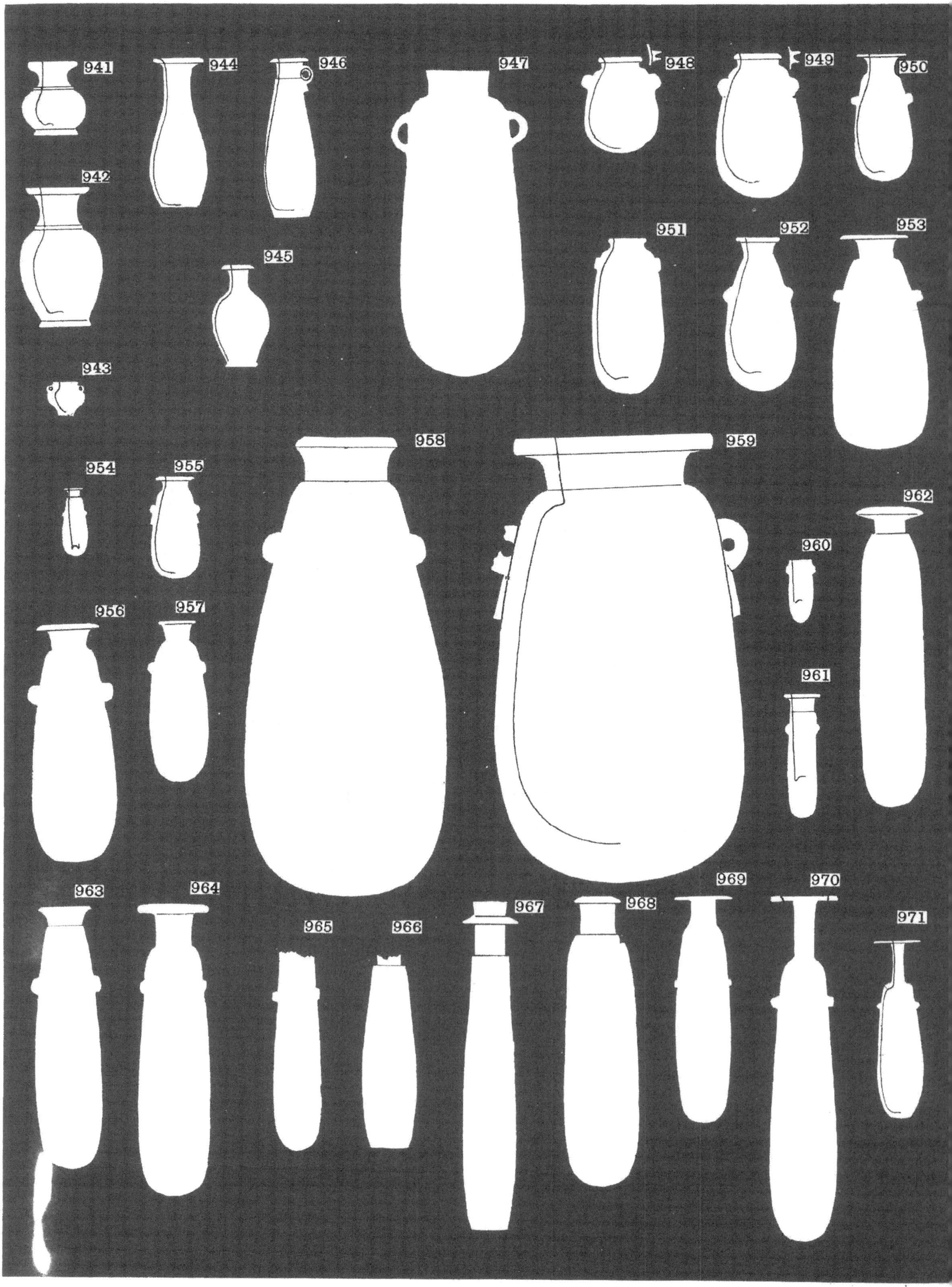
941
942
943
944
945
946
947
948
949
950
951
952
953
954
955
956
957
958
959
960
961
962
963
964
965
966
967
968
969
970
971

972
973
974
975
976
977
978
979
980
981
982
983
984
985
986
987
988
989
990
991
992
993
994
995
996
997

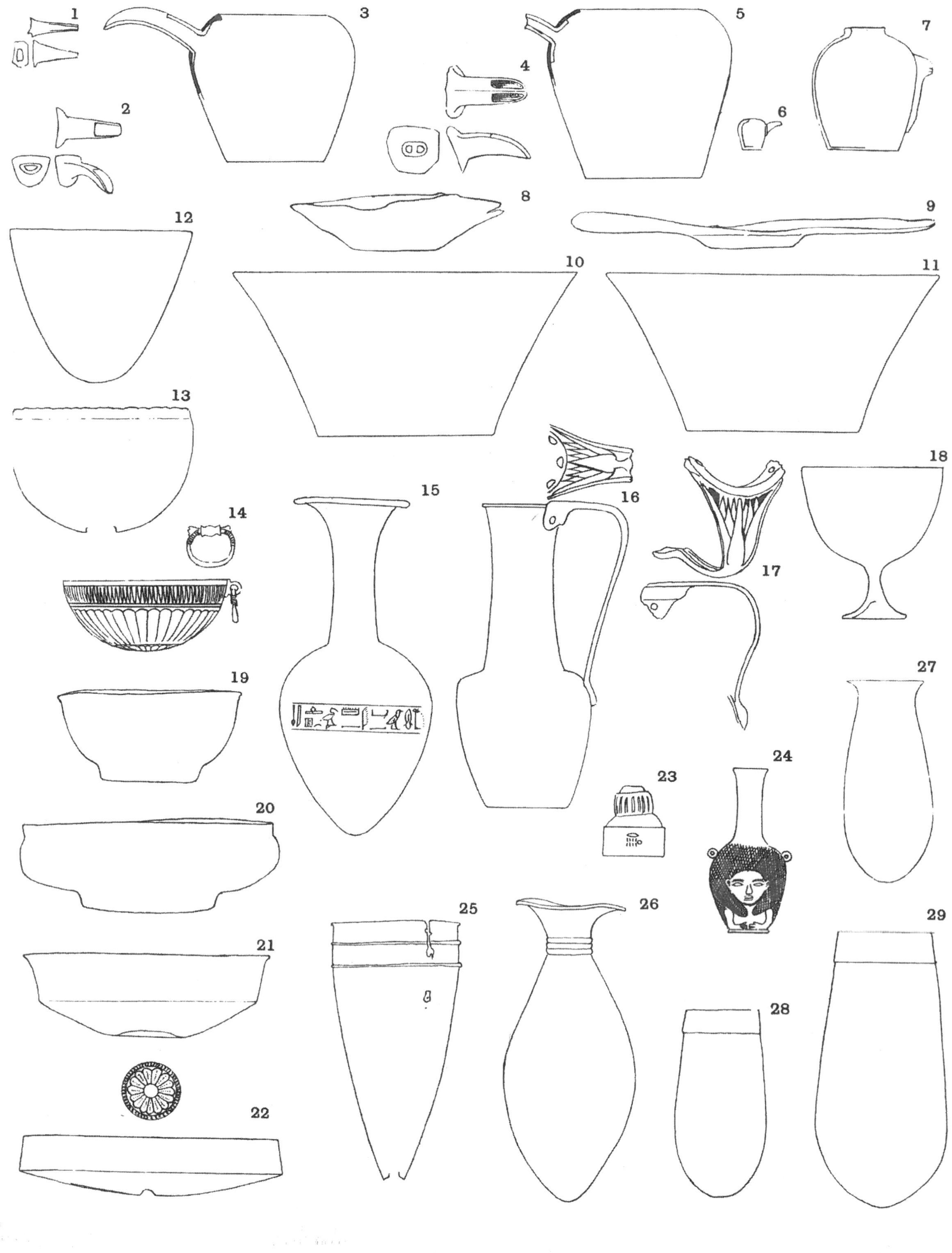
1
2
3
4
5
6
7
8
9
10
11
12
13
14
15
16
17
18
19
20
21
22
23
24
25
26
27
28
29

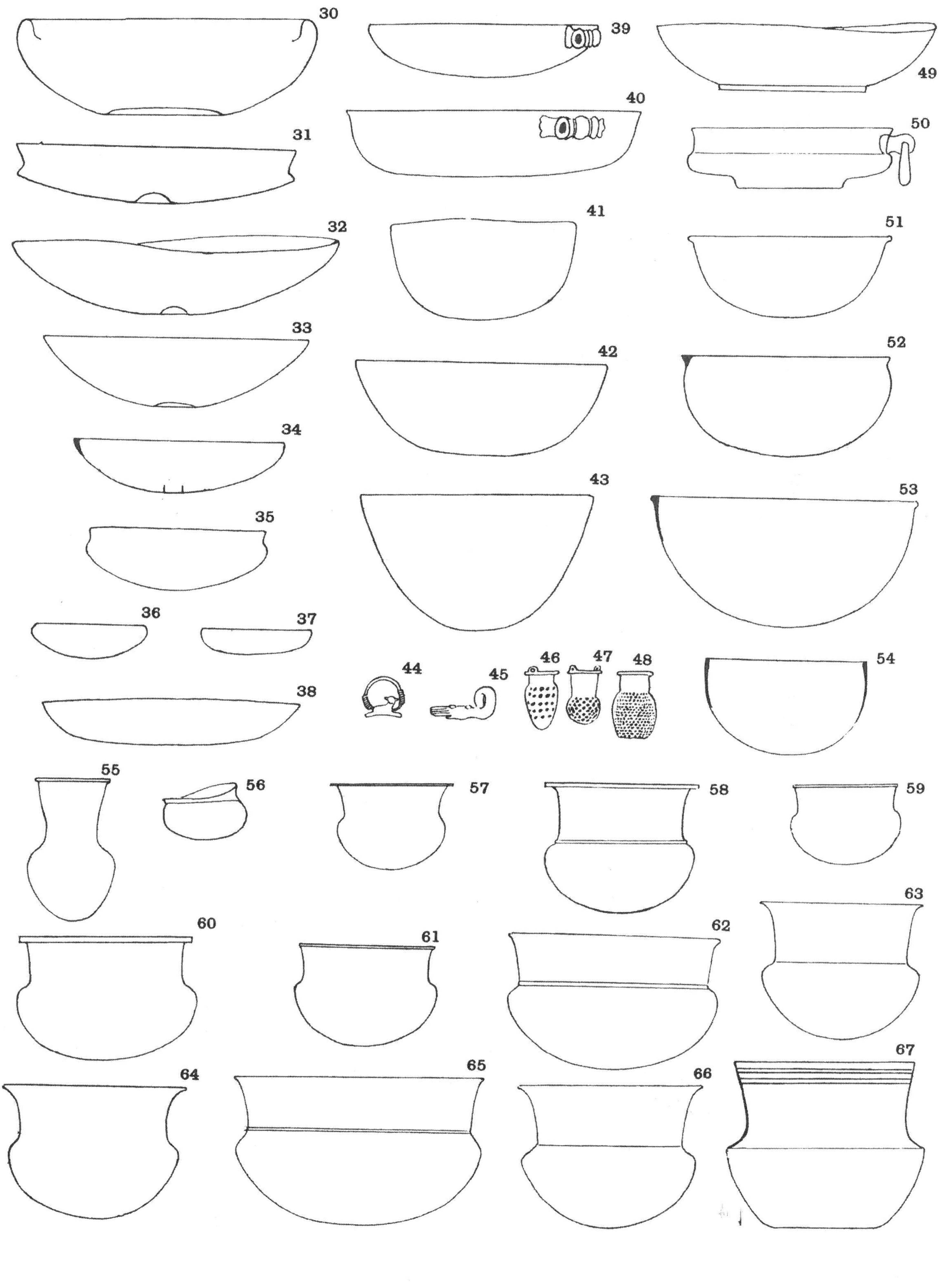
30
31
32
33
34
35
36
37
38
39
40
41
42
43
44
45
46
47
48
49
50
51
52
53
54
55
56
57
58
59
60
61
62
63
64
65
66
67

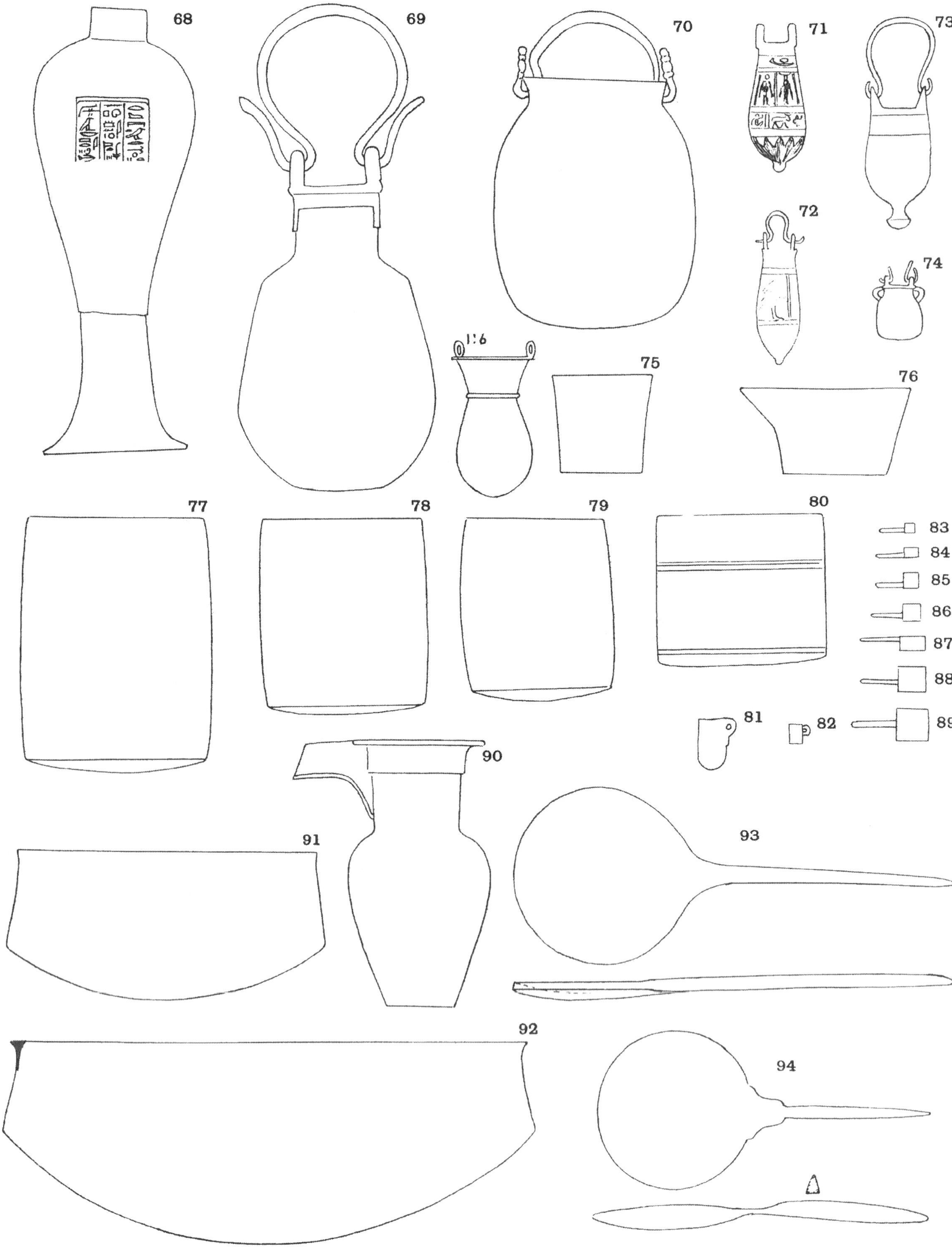
68
69
70
71
73
72
74
1:6
75
76
77
78
79
80
83
84
85
86
87
88
81
82
89
90
91
93
92
94

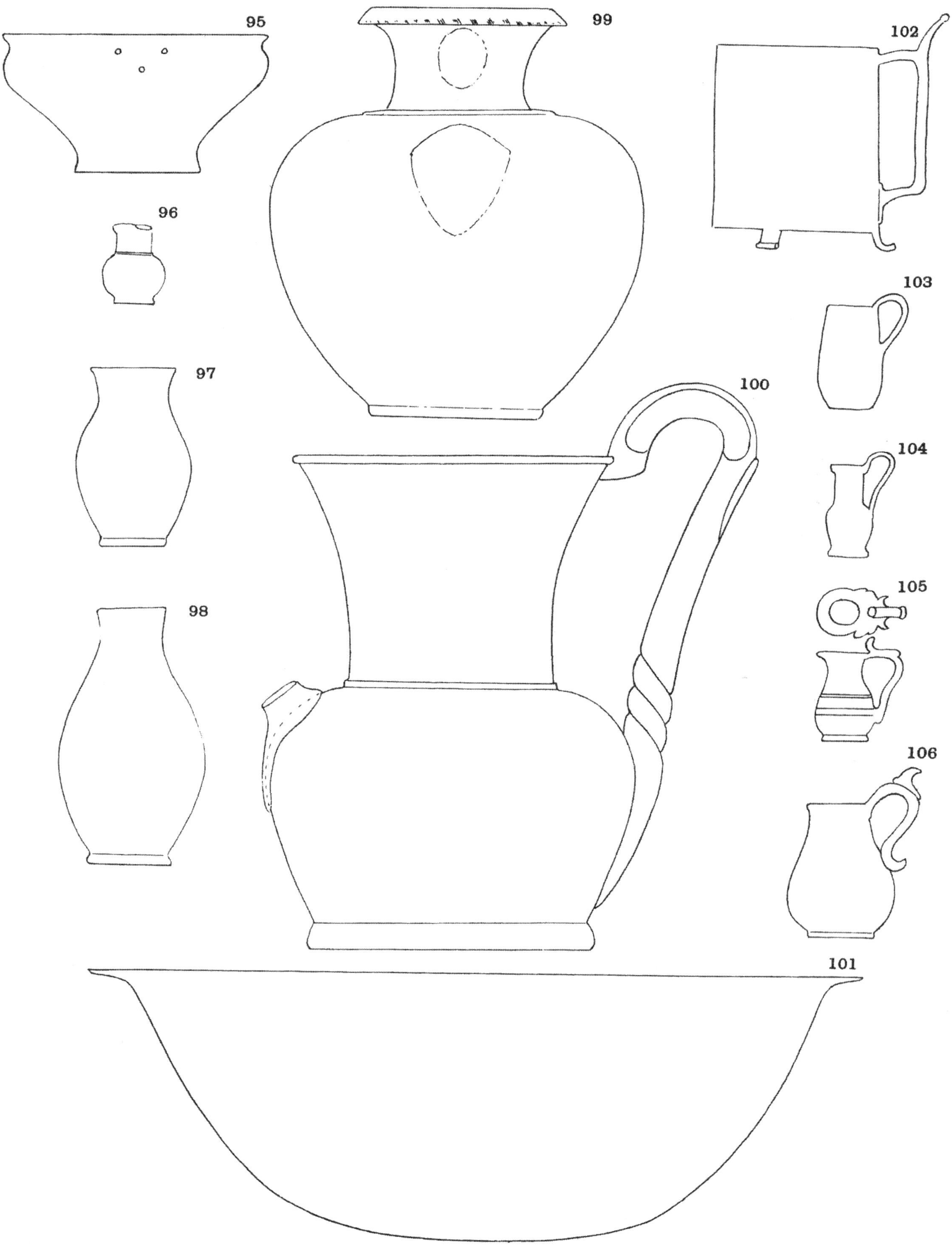
95
96
97
98
99
100
101
102
103
104
105
106

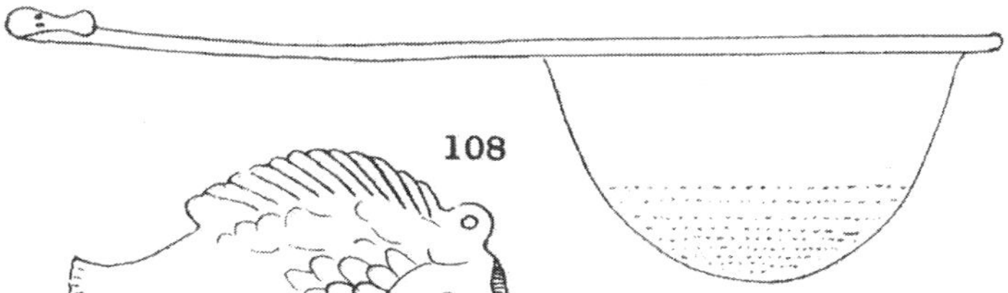

107

110

108

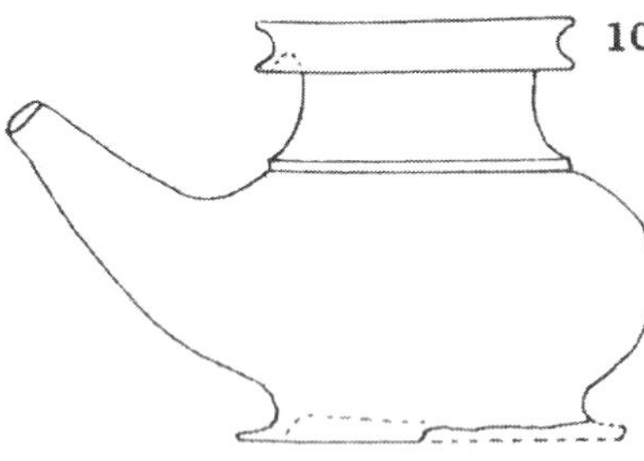

109

111

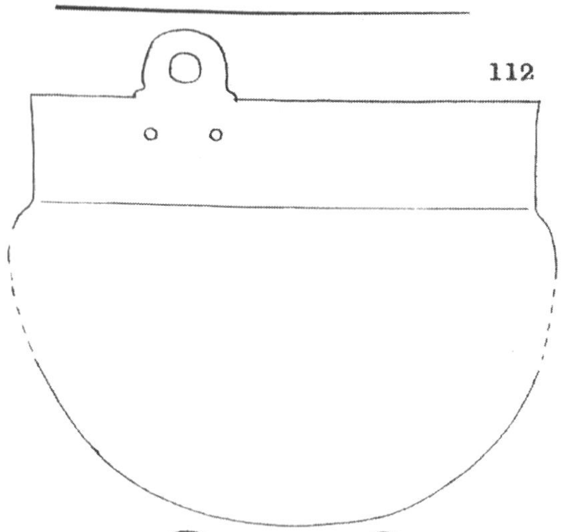

112

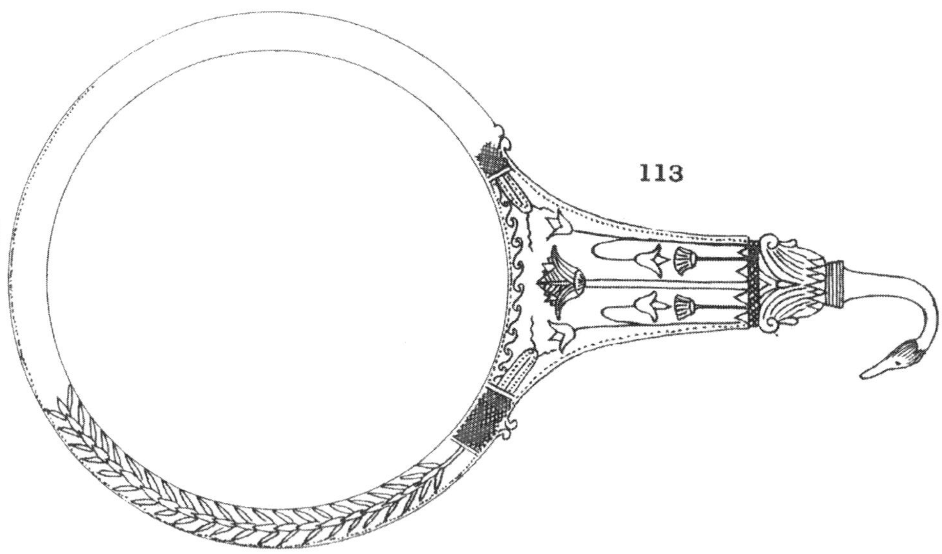

113

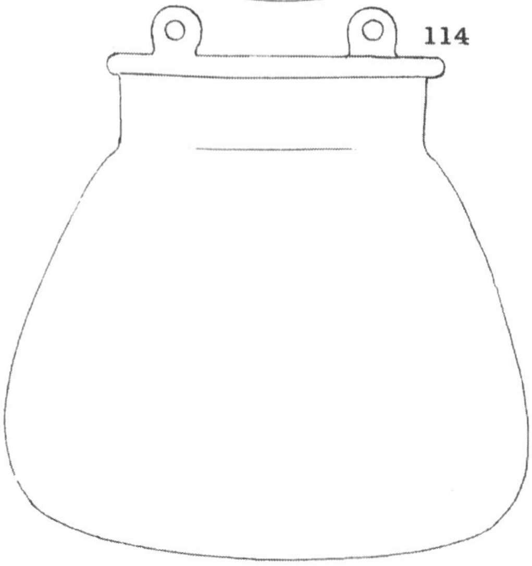

114

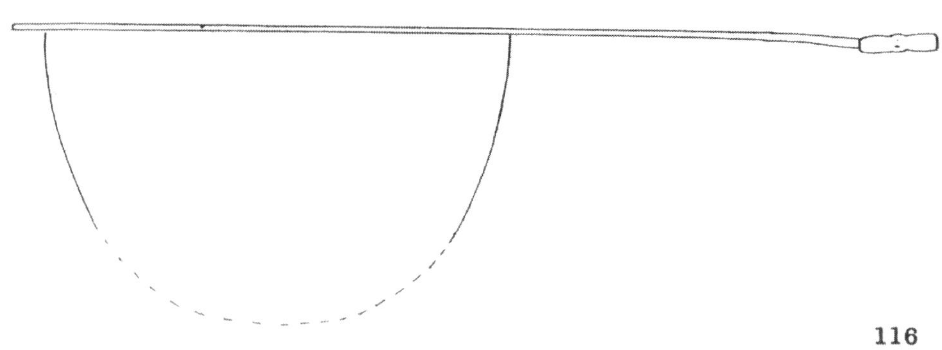

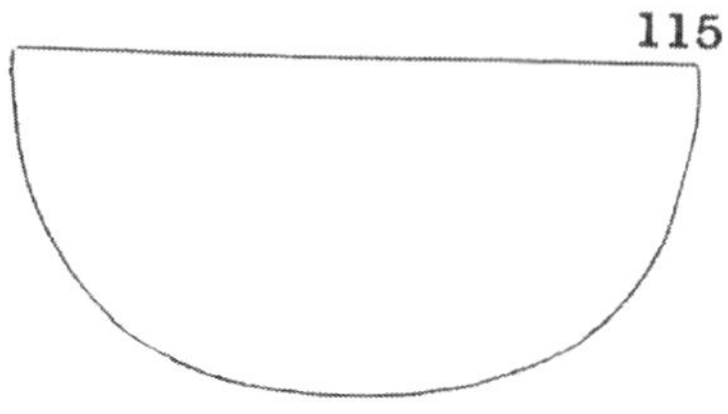

115

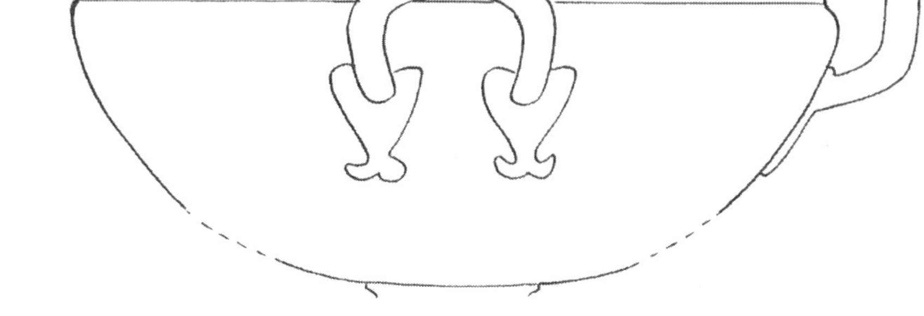

116

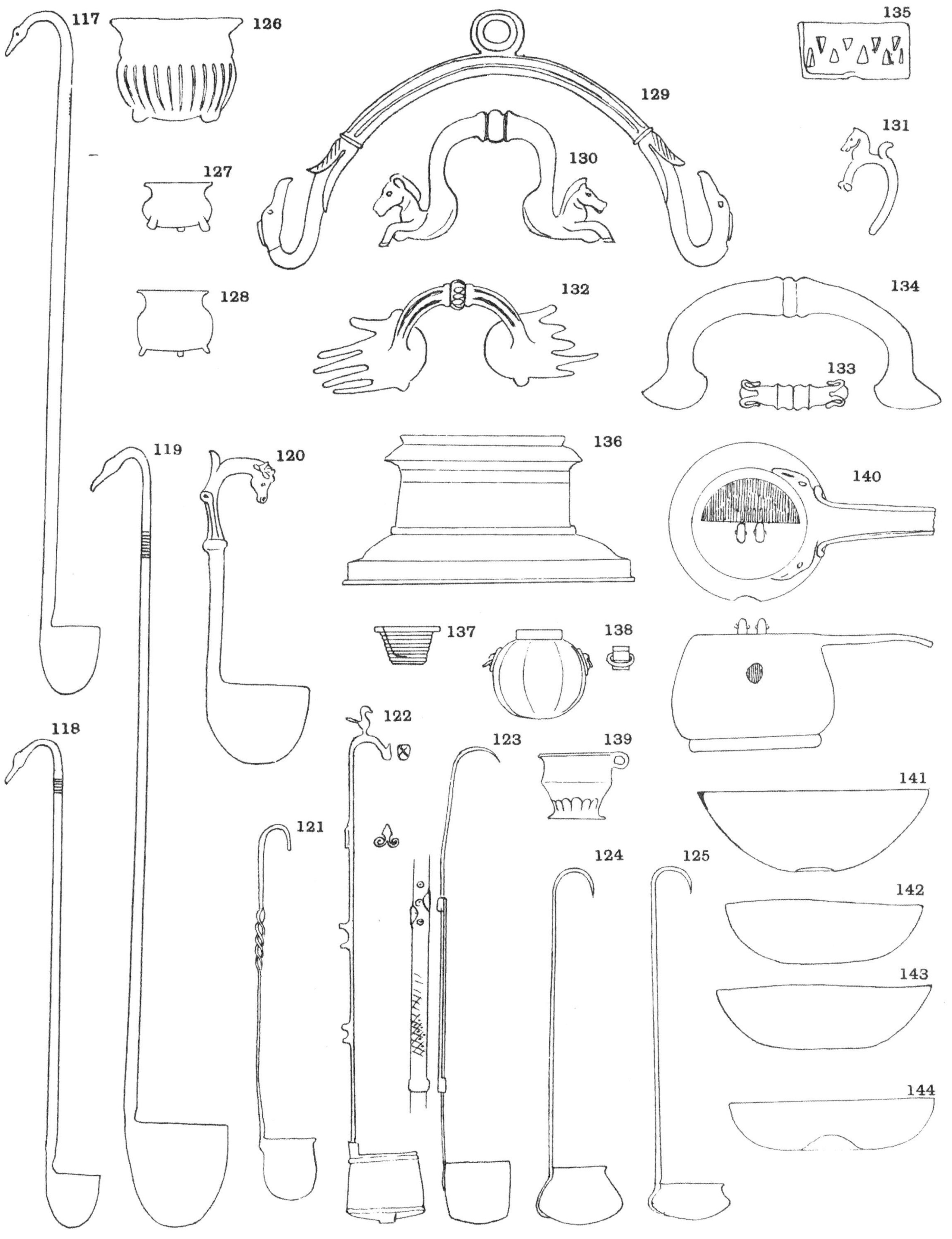
117
126
129
135
131
127
130
128
132
134
133
119
120
136
140
137
138
118
122
123
139
141
121
124
125
142
143
144

1 liquid, "foreign".
2 cup, 1/3 hen 9½ c.i., 1168 c.i., 2300 c.i.
3
4 milk, wine. skin
5 beer. "stone vase"
6 "of Syrian work".
7 cup
8 measure 16 c.i. double handful small
9 for blood, water. to grind
10 beer. to pour out.
11 lotus cup.
12 beer. to water.
13 libation altar
14
15
16 SYRIAN MARIS = 1850 c.i.
17 vessels of silver
18 measure of incense and beer.
19 for eye kohl
20 golden
21 III Sek. III Med IV ii 87 V ii 70 XII ii 147 Khosekhmui copper
22 unguent
23 drunkenness
24 plate L.D. ii, 69
25 hen 29 c.i.
26 honnu 117 c.i.
27 283 c.i. lake
28 or basin, lake
29 Sek. Med. offering
30 var.
31
32 Med. ointment, one of 7 oils
33 oil
34 1/3 hon. leather bottle 9½ cub. in
35 V S.M. XVIII V ii 69
36 or, Paonkhy ointment χους?
37 Med. Sek.
38 grain pot
39 cooking pot
40
41 some of κεραμιον, 1610 c.i.
42 water jug, brewing. beer jug
43 wine
44
45 vase persea.
46 brewing wine
47 horn offering dish
48 ampulla, oil for lamp 128 c.i.
49 libation vase
50 vessel,
51 "servant of the ka"
52 Liquid measure. Liquid
53 Large, flat dish
54 largeness, quantity. beer pot large
55 cauldron, pot
56 metal jug, measure digit.
57 an offering.
58 Med. Sek. measure
59 beer.
60 patera, cup شرب